VOLUME 1 • JANUARY TO APRIL

COUNCIL FIRE

DAILY DEVOTIONALS FROM INDIGENOUS FOLLOWERS OF JESUS

Council Fire: Volume 1

Copyright © 2024 Indian Life Books

In association with the Native Evangelical Fellowship of Canada (NEFC)

All rights reserved. No part of this publication may be reproduced without permission.

Editors: Kene Jackson, Todd Wawrzyniak, Krystal Wawrzyniak;
Copy Editor: Rollie Hodgman; Design and layout: Robin Black.

Scripture quotations are from: Amplified Bible (AMP), Common English Bible (CEB), Easy-to-Read Version (ERV), King James Version (KJV), Modern English Version (MEV), New American Standard Bible (NASB), New English Translation (NET), New International Version (NIV), New King James Version (NKJV), New Living Translation (NLT).

ISBN: 979-8-218-27318-7

Printed in Manitoba, Canada

INTRODUCTION

Welcome to *Council Fire: Volume One*! With all three volumes, *Council Fire* includes 366 devotionals ... one for every day of the year!

Each devotional is written by one of over 40 Indigenous followers of Jesus, representing more than 15 First Nations from over a dozen Canadian provinces and US states. At the back of the book you will find a short introduction to each of our contributing writers.

The Bible is filled with stories of how the Lord worked through the lives of people for His glory. As you read the Scriptures on each page together with the related experiences and thoughts of our writers, may *Council Fire* help bring you closer to our Creator Jesus Christ and the life He desires for each of us ... every day of the year!

You will notice that we have also included a schedule for reading the entire Bible in one year. Really, we need all of Scripture, and reading the whole Bible takes us to places we may not usually go, allowing us to see the big picture of God's plan, reflecting on His character ... 366 days of the year!

JANUARY 1

Plugged In

"The Sovereign LORD is my strength; he makes my feet like the feet of a deer, he enables me to tread on the heights." Habakkuk 3:19 (NIV)

The power was off here at our country home for a few hours this morning. No lights, no coffee, no phone charger, no Calgary News on TV (no TV!), no heat, no nothing! The obvious solution? Drive 30 km to the nearest town for breakfast, hang around and wait for the repair guys to do their thing! Bacon and eggs should help dull the pain.

It got me thinking about how dependent we are on electricity for a power source, and how "hamstrung" we can get when it's not there! Life just sort of grinds to a standstill (if you don't count the bacon and eggs). It seems like everything in our lives has to plug in somewhere!

Our spiritual lives have a similar dynamic; they need to be plugged in! Spiritually, we are powerless to follow God in our own strength; we're like disconnected appliances that don't work without electricity. Living God's way is impossible without God's help. I guess that's something we all need to learn. Once this realization kicks in, we start to trust the Lord for the strength to truly live for Him!

"The LORD is my strength and my shield; my heart trusted in Him, and I am helped; therefore, my heart greatly rejoices, and with my song I will praise Him. The LORD is their strength, and He is the saving refuge of His anointed." Psalm 28:7-8 (NKJV)

– Kene Jackson

Daily Bible Reading Plan: Genesis 1-3; Matthew 1

JANUARY 2

Fearfully & Wonderfully Made

"For you formed my inward parts; You covered me in my mother's womb. I will praise You, for I am fearfully and wonderfully made. Marvelous are Your works, and that my soul knows very well." Psalm 139:13-14 (NKJV)

King David, who wrote this psalm, was overwhelmed by God's awesome creation in the womb. God knew everything about David. In Psalm 139:1-12, scripture indicates that God knew everything that David was doing and going to do—such as sitting down, resting, or when he was traveling.

God knew what David was going to say before the words came out of his mouth. No wonder he was so overwhelmed with God's awesome power, close presence, knowledge, and creation that he had to give God all the praise!

There is no doubt that God's presence is always with us, even before we were born. This whole chapter of Psalm 139 speaks about God who created us . . . fearfully and wonderfully.

The teenage years can be a difficult time. For me, I had trouble accepting who I was and what I looked like. I did not like my dark skin color, dark eyes and hair. I did not view myself as anyone special. Oftentimes I felt that I was overlooked and ignored.

Yet, when I first put my trust in Jesus Christ as my Lord and Savior, these scripture verses spoke directly to my heart. God's Word helped me to see who I really am . . . fearfully and wonderfully made by Him. It did not matter how I looked on the outside—whether I had dark skin, eyes and hair—the important thing was my relationship with Jesus.

As a result of learning this beautiful truth, God showed me that I was seen by Him right from the start! Now I am thankful for the way that God has created me . . . dark skin, hair, eyes and all!

– Myrna Kopf

Daily Bible Reading Plan: Genesis 4-6; Matthew 2

JANUARY 3

Are You Living in the Past, Present or Future?

"Therefore do not worry about tomorrow, for tomorrow will worry about itself. Each day has enough trouble of its own." Matthew 6:34 (NIV)

I have found there are many people who are not living for today. That includes me, at times. The enemy would love for us to live either in the past or in the future.

It is so easy to live in the past, and we could be living with much regret . . . "If only I did it this way; if only I didn't do that." You can be so busy thinking about what you did or didn't do. This is the tactic of the enemy so that we aren't doing what the Lord wants us to be doing today. If you are feeling that way, and you have children, you are missing out on what they are doing today. You could be missing out on helping them to choose the Lord and His way.

It's just as easy to be living in the future. You know . . . "When I get more money, or when I get a better job, or when I can do things better." Now, I firmly believe that it's good to have goals—because if you don't have any goals, how can you aim for something? But sometimes we find ourselves worrying about tomorrow and what it will bring. I remember one time my husband saying to me, "Why worry when you can pray?" My thought at that time was, "How can I pray while I'm worrying?" Now I fully agree with him!

Don't let the worries of this world control you to a point that you are not present for the people around you. You will not be present for God to use you. You will miss out on so much of what God is trying to teach you and His blessings. Live your life to the fullest today!

– Pat Hall

Daily Bible Reading Plan: Genesis 7-9; Matthew 3

JANUARY 4

Be Filled with the Spirit

"I am the vine; you are the branches. He who abides in Me, and I in him, bears much fruit; for without Me you can do nothing." John 15:5 (NKJV)

How do we know if a person is filled with God's Holy Spirit? What should we look for? We cannot see the way God sees, and we may not come to a proper conclusion. However, God does give us wise counsel. We are to look at the fruits of his or her life. Galatians 5:22-23a (NKJV) says: "The fruit of the Spirit is love, joy, peace, longsuffering, kindness, goodness, faithfulness, gentleness, self-control."

A fruit tree is an example. While the sap is filling the tree, you and I may not notice much difference—we may not even know what kind of fruit tree it is until the fruit appears. Galatians 5:16 (NKJV) says, "Walk in the Spirit." This is the continual submission to God that will result in fruit bearing of the Spirit through you. Receiving the power of the Spirit (or the anointing, as it is sometimes referred to) is not possible without submission to the Lord.

There are no short cuts—it is still dying to the old self life and being led by the Spirit of God. Jesus said, "I am the Vine." If the branch is detached from the main source of its water supply, it will wither. So it is with the believer. You cannot live a victorious Christian life, or help others to know the Lord, unless you abide (live close) to Jesus Christ.

Spirit-led Paul was concerned about his walk with the Lord. First Corinthians 9:27 (NKJV) says: "But I discipline my body and bring it into subjection, lest, when I have preached to others, I myself should become disqualified." Paul was not thinking of being lost again but being disqualified in his service for the Lord.

Lord, I want to be filled with your Spirit. Please teach me.

– Bill Jackson

Daily Bible Reading Plan: Genesis 10-12; Matthew 4

JANUARY 5

Space Travel

"Do you not know? Have you not heard? The LORD is the everlasting God, the Creator of the ends of the earth." Isaiah 40:28a (NIV)

Do you ever feel tired or a little dizzy? It might have something to do with our space travels. We ride on a spinning planet, traveling over 24,000 miles each day (at the equator) at a speed of 1,000 miles per hour. At the same time, we journey around our sun for a year at a speed of over 67,000 miles per hour, completing a tour of 92,960,000 miles. As we rotate on our axis and revolve in orbit around our sun, we stay in tandem with the other planets in our solar system as our Milky Way galaxy circles among our super-cluster of galaxies rotating throughout the universe.

Gravity holds us attached to the planet so we don't fall off. But it seems that with all this spinning, we should fling off into space. Not only do we stay on our super amusement park ride, but our moon stays right with us, helping us to stay in proper rotation, moving our tides and illuminating our night journeys.

This frenetic traveling may explain why we get tired, but it doesn't explain how we can move such great distances at astronomical speeds . . . and then go about our business as if we were in complete control. People work to change time (daylight savings time). People work to try to control the climate. I would not blame anyone for being nervous about life on earth, but I think about the real reason we are on this planet. It helps me see my life in perspective to the One who "holds all things together" (Colossians 1:17).

Dear Jesus, I have no idea how You hold our universe together. Please increase my knowledge of who You are and open my heart's understanding of Your invitation to me to be a part of Your kingdom today and forever.

– Sue Carlisle

Daily Bible Reading Plan: Genesis 13-15

JANUARY 6

Growing in the Lord

"But grow in grace, and in the knowledge of our Lord and Savior Jesus Christ. To Him be glory both now and forever. Amen." 2 Peter 3:18 (KJV)

I remember when I first came to Jesus. I was 16 years old and didn't have a clue of how to follow the Lord! Over the years I learned many things about living for Jesus. I want to share with you the three biggest things that have helped me grow in my walk.

(1) Getting into God's Word. At first I didn't know much about the Bible and wasn't too interested in getting deeper into it. But that is the way the Lord speaks to us. It's only when I began to read and understand the Bible that I grew in my faith. It's now a part of everyday life.

(2) Praying. I love to pray now, but it wasn't always that way. I didn't understand the importance of open communication with God. At first, I would run out of things to pray after five minutes. As my relationship with the Lord got deeper, I found that I could talk to Him about absolutely anything!

(3) Making the Right Choices. Before a person becomes a believer, the Lord is not part of their decision making. That's how it was for me. Then His Word began to come alive to me and was what I would base my choices on. God's Word helped me to realize when I was in the wrong, and I came under the Holy Spirit's conviction when I made selfish choices.

My relationship to God today is the biggest thing in my life. Everything else is secondary to Him! I wouldn't want it to be any other way.

Dear God, thank You that when I become anxious and worried, I can always come to You. You are faithful and have shown me that I can leave my burdens and cares with You. Amen.

– Milly Jackson

Daily Bible Reading Plan: Genesis 16-17; Matthew 5

JANUARY 7

Living Out God's Promises

"Honor thy father and mother; which is the first commandment with promise; that it may be well with thee, and thou mayest live long on the earth." Ephesians 6:2-3 (KJV)

The Bible is full of God's wonderful promises for us to obey and reap His blessings. Exodus 20:12 is another scripture that instructs us to honor our parents—with a similar promise. For the most part, it was natural for me to love and honor my parents. But there was a time in my life I struggled, as I wanted to go my own way. It began when I left home to attend residential school and later, high school.

This is where I was exposed to ungodliness. I believe it was the prayers of my parents that kept me alive. After high school I made the decision to follow the Lord, and it was a blessing to be a part of a Bible-believing church where I was discipled. Living out God's Word became more meaningful, and I was still guided by my Christian parents, as our relationship became God based.

Moving forward, my parents reached their time to retire, and I became the main caregiver. It was both an honor and the most challenging task to fulfill until they both succumbed to illnesses. My mother was 84 years old when she died of heart failure, and my father was 86 when he died of cancer. It is never easy to watch loved ones suffer, but the quality time we spent together outweighs the pain. I will forever treasure the memories of my time with them.

Today, I thank my heavenly Father for the opportunity and strength He gave to be a part of honoring my parents. He is faithful, and He will always fulfil His promises written in His Word. In my role as a mental health counselor, I get to encourage others to do their best when given the opportunity to look after their parents. Truly it is an honor.

– Liz Beardy

Daily Bible Reading Plan: Genesis 18-19; Matthew 6

JANUARY 8

Storms

"When you go through deep waters, I will be with you. When you go through rivers of difficulty, you will not drown. When you walk through the fire of oppression, you will not be burned up; the flames will not consume you." Isaiah 43:2 (NLT)

I was watching a news report this morning about an earthquake in Asia. It wasn't as bad as some earthquakes, but it got me thinking about the "storms" we all face in life. Everybody has their share of storms—storms of health, relationships, finances, employment (or lack thereof) . . . storms of scenarios we didn't choose, and then the "reap what you sow" quagmires we find ourselves in.

God's Word gives us answers to the storms we face in this life. Everything from attitude struggles to marriage breakdown, from noisy neighbors to out-of-control credit cards—you get the picture . . . everything!

You or I might not be too thrilled sometimes about the answers we find in God's Word, but that's not the point. God's Word is the truth, and the truth doesn't change.

Storms come whether we deserve them or not—that's just how life goes. God's Word has the answer to each tempest. It's up to us to apply those principles and parameters to the life scenarios we find ourselves or put ourselves in. Our response to the storm is in our hands.

– Kene Jackson

Daily Bible Reading Plan: Genesis 20-22

JANUARY 9

Running from God

"But Jonah arose to flee to Tarshish from the presence of the LORD. He went down to Joppa, and found a ship going to Tarshish; so he paid the fare, and went down into it, to go with them to Tarshish from the presence of the LORD." Jonah 1:3 (NKJV)

A few years ago at our Kikino Family Bible Camp, one of our dogs was sniffing in a small white garbage bag, and his head got caught in the handle. He took off running for his life, as the bag was following him wherever he went! He was scared and running in all directions. Finally, after calling our dog multiple times, he came so I could rescue him.

This incident has always stuck in my memory for various reasons. Many people run from many things in their lives, and they can run from those things for many years. They can run from painful hurts of the past that are difficult to work through. However, God can heal all pains, and the running can stop.

Then there are those people who are running from God because they are unwilling to surrender an area of their lives or unwilling to obey a calling from God for their lives. The psalmist David wondered about where he could run from God—since God was everywhere at the same time.

The prophet Jonah had a specific calling to his enemies, and his unwillingness to obey that call set off a sequence of events that finally brought him to a place of humility and obedience. Truly we can never run away from God. Instead of running from Him, let us run to Him like the Prodigal Son (see Luke 15:11-31) running back to his father. What are you running from? When will you stop running? Will you run to the Lord?

Lord, enable me to run to You in all of life's struggles and problems. Amen.

— Frank Ward

Daily Bible Reading Plan: Genesis 23-24; Matthew 7

JANUARY 10

Jacob's Favoritism

"Now Israel (Jacob) loved Joseph more than all his children, because he was the son of his old age; and he made him a coat of many colors. And when his brethren saw that their father loved him more than all his brethren, they hated him, and could not speak peaceably unto him." Genesis 37:3-4 (KJV, clarification added)

We see that Jacob practiced favoritism. This show of affection for one boy from a large family did not help the brothers in their attitude toward the favored one.

There is no excuse for sin at any time, but there are also actions that can be offensive, and could hinder a person from coming to the Lord. Joseph's testimony was not received by most of his brothers, who treated him rudely and sold him into slavery.

This problem of favoritism showed up again when the brothers came with the coat of many colors, which had been dipped in blood. Note Genesis 37:32: *"Your son's* coat"—not *our brother's* coat—as it might have been said.

Ask God to give you love for *all* the children in your house, and be sure you teach them God's way, even if it is not the practice in your community. Being fair to all members of the family is God's way, and you will see that God's way is always best.

"Then Peter opened his mouth and said: 'in truth I perceive that God shows no partiality'" Acts 10:34 (NKJV).

– Bill Jackson

Daily Bible Reading Plan: Genesis 25-26

JANUARY 11

Clay Pots

"For God, who said, 'Let light shine out of darkness,' made his light shine in our hearts to give us the light of the knowledge of the glory of God in the face of Christ. But we have this treasure in jars of clay to show that this all-surpassing power is from God and not from us. We are hard pressed on every side, but not crushed; perplexed, but not in despair; persecuted, but not abandoned; struck down, but not destroyed." 2 Corinthians 4:6-9 (NIV)

God called Gideon to save Israel from the Midianites. Gideon started with 32,000 men, but that was too many for God's purpose, so He reduced them down to 300 men. The victory would come through God's power—not their own. God wanted His people to trust Him and shine. Gideon divided the men into three groups; each carried a trumpet and a hidden torch inside a clay pot. Upon command, they blew their trumpets and broke their jars and let the light pour out. The enemy believed that each trumpet and light had thousands of troops behind it, so they panicked and turned on each other.

My pot's artistic decoration wore off years ago. It carries a few chips now, and a crack runs part way down one side. I pray that God's light will shine through the brokenness. I thought of Romans 8:28: "And we know that in all things God works for the good of those who love him, who have been called according to his purpose." (NIV) A potter's hands work the clay, shaping and forming it to fit his purpose.

Dear Father, thank You for working out the lumps of my transgressions so that You can form me into the image of Christ according to Your purpose. Please give me insight and understanding from Your Word and Your Holy Spirit so that I can take advantage of difficult times and use them as an opportunity to share Your light with others.

– Sue Carlisle

Daily Bible Reading Plan: Genesis 27-28; Matthew 8

JANUARY 12

Being an Example

"In the same way, let your light shine before others, so that they may see your good works and give glory to your Father who is in heaven." Matthew 5:16 (ESV)

Our Ladies Bible study is really bolstering my faith and how I see myself as a born-again believer. I admit the enemy was gaining in holding me down. It has been difficult these past two years as I age, and physical problems persist. Yet I remember all that Jesus endured before His death on the cross and I say, "Why not me? Jesus, you went through so much more, this is trivial compared to the pain and suffering you had."

Our study is based on Colossians. We are reminded that our words should be gracious and seasoned with salt to give the unbeliever a reason to hear more and come to Jesus. I have also learned to turn off the accusations, the attempts to burden me with guilt and, most of all, to turn to Jesus every time and acknowledge His strength is sufficient for me in all things. The study book is called *He Is Enough*.

I remember when my husband first came to the Lord. He led singing at fellowship on Sundays, and we had Bible studies in our home. All the learning I had growing up came back and had so much more meaning and brought joy to my heart. Because my husband had become sober through Alcoholics Anonymous, most of the men who came to study were also in the AA program. They liked what they saw and heard in my husband's sharing. Several were men he grew up with in Merritt, B.C., and two accepted Jesus because of his example.

Dear Heavenly Father, may we always shine for You so others will be attracted to You.

– Loretta Oppenheim

Daily Bible Reading Plan: Genesis 29-30; Matthew 9

JANUARY 13

Trophies

"For where your treasure is, there your heart will be also." Matthew 6:21 (NIV)

"But seek first his kingdom and his righteousness and all these things will be given to you as well." Matthew 6:33 (NIV)

We once had trophies lined up in our house from accomplishments, and we were especially recognized and known for the sport of volleyball. One day, as I was sitting there looking at those trophies, I realized that I, as a father, was missing the whole point if I was raising my children to base their lives only on who they are and what they can be through education and sports.

In Deuteronomy 6:7, the Word of God commands us parents to impress upon the hearts of our children, to talk to them about loving God with all our heart, soul and strength. We thought we had achieved a lot, and yet sin had crept in because I was not alert as a father, a leader, a spiritual protector of our household.

I needed to prepare my family not only for this world, with its presence of evil, but to prepare them ever so greatly to put their trust in Jesus Christ, to follow Him, and walk with Him to enjoy the abundant life by having a close relationship with Jesus Christ.

I started "cleaning" my house. I put aside the gold trophies that get tarnished by time, and I brought out the more important thing: the Word of God. I have never made a better choice. I love my Lord and thank Him for the time He has given me to share what is the most important thing in life.

There are so many distractions in life, even good ones, whether it be music, sports, jobs and security. We can become so busy that we forget our calling from the Lord, to seek first the kingdom of God.

– Ken Mitsuing

Daily Bible Reading Plan: Genesis 31-32

JANUARY 14

The Message and the Method

"YOU WILL BE MY WITNESSES in Jerusalem, and in all Judea and Samaria, and to the ends of the earth." Acts 1:8 *(NIV, caps my own)*

Time has a way of changing things—well, not everything, but some things. One of the things that sometimes needs to change is the way we do ministry. I remember back in the early 1980s, reading some of the writings of NEFC Founder, Tom Francis, and his successor, Joseph Jolly.

There was a section in our NEFC objectives that said: "NEFC yearns to share the Gospel in every Native community in Canada." My unspoken thought at the time was, "Yeah, right! That's just dreamy. It's not reality! How could we ever reach a goal like that?"

In the early 2000s, NEFC's radio broadcast "Christ Jesus the Light (CJTL)" was born. As time went on, it became more and more of a gospel tool that has been used effectively for Jesus. When we added internet audio broadcasting several years later, it became globally accessible. Anyplace that has internet can now tune in to the 24-hour, 365-days-a-year gospel programming that CJTL offers! About 90% of our Native communities can now get nonstop gospel broadcasting! (That's besides the 28 communities that have a local CJTL FM radio broadcast.)

The words that were penned back in the early 1970s are becoming reality many years later! The message hasn't changed, only the methods.

– Kene Jackson

Daily Bible Reading Plan: Genesis 33-35; Matthew 10

JANUARY 15

Never Saw It Coming

"The steadfast love of the Lord never ceases, his mercies never come to an end; they are new every morning; great is your faithfulness." Lamentations 3:22-23 (ESV)

When my father passed away in 2019, it was the first time in my parents' 57 years of marriage that my mother would be alone. We had assured my father not to worry, that my four brothers and one sister and I would take care of her.

We were all taught that in the first year we should let the grieving grieve. So, we let our mother do that and, like we promised our dad, we were there for her. In 2020, I started to notice a change in my mom. I didn't think much of it, but the signs became clearer. In 2022, my mom was diagnosed with dementia. At first, we didn't know what to expect, and it was hard learning how this neurological disease was robbing our mother of her memory.

This was a very dark time of my life, as the woman who I have always looked up to was slowly disappearing. In the beginning I cried many nights, almost becoming consumed in grief. During those times I cried out to the Lord to help my family and I through the journey we were about to take.

Now, as I awake in the mornings after a year of her diagnosis, I am thankful that my mother is still with us, in spite of her illness. I am also thankful that, because of her own faith, someday she will become whole again in reunion with my dad and the loved ones that have gone before her—in the presence of God Himself.

This illness has reminded me to lean on God for His strength. He has never left us, and we continue trusting in His love. This is not the end, but the beginning of something beautiful. Today I just continue to keep trusting God's faithful love for us.

– Laurie Wood Ducharme

Daily Bible Reading Plan: Genesis 36-38

JANUARY 16

The God We Serve

"Hear me, LORD, and answer me, for I am poor and needy."
Psalm 86:1 (NIV)

"Do not be deceived, God is not mocked; for whatever a man sows, that he will also reap." Galatians 6:7 (NKJV)

The God of the Bible is a God of love, mercy and justice. I gave up trying to understand God a long time ago because His ways are far higher than ours (Isaiah 55:8-9). Both my wife and I came to know Christ in 1979 as a result of a terrible tragedy in my brother and sister-in law's lives. Their five-year-old son drowned in a small creek in central Winnipeg.

God spoke to me "loud and clear" about my own life and the direction I was going. I was definitely on the road to hell and destruction. But the good news! God took that tragedy and turned it around for the good—not only for my family, but many other family members and friends, as well. Romans 8:28 says, "All things work together for the good to those who love God and have been called according to His purpose." (NET)

I don't know where you are at today, but I ask you to seriously consider the God of love, mercy, and justice as your personal Savior by receiving His Son Jesus. He died for our sins; but He also rose again to give us victory over our sins. Simply pray, "God, I am lost in sin, please forgive me of all my sins and shortcomings in life; I turn away from that lifestyle now and receive you as my Lord and Savior. Amen."

If you have prayed the above prayer ... or one similar ... Welcome to the family of God! I encourage you to get a Bible and begin reading it. Get into a community with people who teach the Bible. Seek to make Christian friends and meet regularly for encouragement, support, and prayer. And start sharing your faith with people whom God sends your way.

– Marshall Murdock

Daily Bible Reading Plan: Genesis 39-40; Matthew 11

JANUARY 17

Pontius Pilate Stands His Ground

"The chief priests of the Jews said to Pilate, the Roman Governor, 'Do not write, "The King of the Jews," but, "He said I am the King of the Jews." ' Pilate answered, 'What I have written, I have written.'"
John 19:21-22 (NKJV)

When asked, "Why do you believe in the white man's God?" by those who reject Christianity, many if not most Native/Indigenous Christians may feel a level of discomfort. The long history of mistreatment of Native peoples by Euro-Americans on many levels speaks for itself, and many still feel the psychological lashes of that brutal and unfortunate era.

In Native communities, Native Christians may find themselves being treated (subtly or outwardly) as traitors to their cultures. Witnessing—telling others about God and the sacrifice Jesus made for the redemption of all who believe in His divinity—can be especially difficult under such circumstances.

But, although Pontius Pilate, the Roman governor (an unbeliever as far as we know) was shouted down when he tried to save Jesus from the mob that called for his crucifixion, he stood his ground: "Why? What evil has He done?" He pleads to a crowd that was crying out for Jesus's death all the louder. Standing his ground, Pilate risked losing the support of the chief priests and possibly other Romans when he retorted, "What I have written, I have written."

When challenged by others when sharing our faith, we believers must stand as well!

Father God, in the Name of Jesus, I ask that You be with me in my moments of trial. Help me to hold on to Your promise that You will never leave me or forsake me. And having done all . . . stand.

– Kiki BelMonte-Schaller

Daily Bible Reading Plan: Genesis 41-42; Matthew 12

JANUARY 18

Do Not Hinder the Children

"Jesus said, 'Let the children alone, and do not hinder them from coming to Me; for the kingdom of heaven belongs to such as these.'" Matthew 19:14 (NASB)

I can remember when a certain woman came to me. She was very distraught. She told me that her grandson had just been born, and she had been told to go find a priest to baptize her grandson, or else he would go to hell. I told her that, as a pastor, I don't do water baptisms for babies. I told her what I do is called a "dedication" to the Lord, and we wouldn't have to rush right into it.

She was surprised that I said this. I told her that in Scripture Jesus Himself was dedicated. I also told her if her grandchild would die as an infant, he would be accepted into the kingdom by Jesus himself. So I told her not to worry, and that I could dedicate her grandchild. She said thank you and walked away. I am not sure what she did because I did not hear from her again.

This is what Scripture says in Luke 2:21-23 (NLT): "Eight days later, when the baby was circumcised, he was named Jesus, the name given him by the angel even before he was conceived. Then it was time for their purification offering, as required by the law of Moses after the birth of a child; so his parents took him to Jerusalem to present him to the Lord. The law of the Lord says, 'If a woman's first child is a boy, he must be dedicated to the LORD.'"

It is written that Jesus was dedicated after birth, and it would be great if all babies could be given this opportunity—to be dedicated to the Lord by parents who follow Jesus.

– Kirby James

Daily Bible Reading Plan: Genesis 43-45

JANUARY 19

Run the Race You Know You Can't Win

"When I fall, I shall arise." Micah 7:8b (KJV)

It doesn't take courage to run the race you know you will win. It takes courage to run the race you know you *can't* win.

When my daughter, Storm, was in school she joined the track team. She was small for her age and she had asthma. She would enter every event and she always came in last . . . and not just "last," but sometimes minutes behind the winner. At times it was painful to watch her struggling to cross the finish line when every breath was an effort.

At one event she was so far behind that the race was not just "over"—people were leaving the bleachers and headed toward their cars before she crossed the finish line. The only people there to cheer for her were her family and the coach.

She ran the race she knew she couldn't win, but she ran anyway and she always finished the race.

She never felt shame or regret; she never felt she had to apologize or explain why she kept running; she never dropped out or quit the team. She would shrug off the loss and say, "Someone has to win the race and someone has to come in last. If I didn't come in last, someone else would be last, and maybe they would feel badly about it. But I don't feel bad. For me, it is enough to just run and feel the wind in my face and my hair and my sneakers hitting the track. That's enough."

Eventually, Storm graduated from university and traveled the world, and every night she runs a mile in a park for the joy of running.

Lord, remind me that I don't have to win worldly races, or even worldly prizes. You love me just as I am.

– Crying Wind

Daily Bible Reading Plan: Genesis 46-48

JANUARY 20

Poverty or Plenty

"I am not saying this because I am in need, for I have learned to be content whatever the circumstances." Philippians 4:11 (NIV)

Have you ever been flat broke? There've been a few times I've been there, and it's not a real enjoyable place to be. At the other end of that gamut is having more than enough, which is a whole lot more comfortable and easier to appreciate!

The Apostle Paul, like most of us, didn't have a whole lot of trouble dealing with the upper end of the "poverty to plenty" spectrum—that wouldn't have been an issue.

Writing to the Philippians about the downer end of that prosperity scale was more where the tires met the tarmac. He might have been referring to some of the Mideast dungeons he'd been a "guest" in on a number of occasions. These were often just a hole in the ground; the food was just what friends and family would come and toss in; it was either bone-chilling wet or sweltering dry, and there were no set release dates. Paul had learned how to handle hard places!

Verse 13 is usually quoted in the broader field of "God strengthening His people for any situation they face." That isn't wrong but, in this context, it focuses on being able to live contentedly and work effectively in this unpredictable "poverty to plenty" life space of the believer's journey.

"I can do all this through him who gives me strength" (Philippians 4:13, NIV). No matter where a person is on the comfort, financial and social registers, our God gives His people the stamina and staying power to be content in whatever scenario life finds them.

– Kene Jackson

Daily Bible Reading Plan: Genesis 49-50; Matthew 13

JANUARY 21

Reconciliation

"Many are the plans in a person's heart; but it is the Lord's purpose that prevails." Proverbs 19:21 (NIV)

In the past few years, much has been said regarding reconciliation between residential school survivors and the government. I held all that rhetoric at arm's length until last year. Two incidents opened up feelings that were hidden away under years of denial and suspicion.

The first incident was the recounting of my Day School experience. Memories of small children housed in a one-room school with rows of desks for grades 1-6. Everything that happened in that room was a common experience. For many of us, it was our first experience with a non-indigenous person. She was very cruel, subjecting us to corporal punishment and inhuman acts such as refusing bathroom privileges, until it was too late for comfort or pride.

The second incident was hearing about the discovery of 200-plus graves in the Kamloops Indian Residential School grounds. I had heard of these stories back while I was in residential school in Williams Lake, but it was an unfathomable horror, so I pushed the thought out of my mind.

I recount these things to give a capsule of the hearts of a broken people needing reconciliation. Even after many years of living the Christian life, I experienced a deep sadness in realizing that human beings can commit such vile acts out of their own selfish desires. Even if their initial purpose was for good, their methods were not godly.

For "true reconciliation," one must first be reconciled to God. Romans 10:9-10 says: "If you confess with your mouth Jesus as Lord, and believe in your heart that God raised Him from the dead, you will be saved; for with the heart a person believes, resulting in righteousness, and with the mouth he confesses, resulting in salvation." (NASB)

God in heaven, I pray for the hurting people of the residential school era. I ask that you would open their spiritual eyes to see You.

– Theresa Bose

Daily Bible Reading Plan: Exodus 1-3; Matthew 14

JANUARY 22

Forgiveness

"And Simon Peter stood and warmed himself. They said therefore unto him, Art not thou also one of his disciples? He denied it, and said, I am not." John 18:25 (KJV)

"If we confess our sins, He is faithful and just to forgive us our sins and to cleanse us from all unrighteousness." 1 John 1:9 (KJV)

Peter had just done the unthinkable! He had denied Jesus and, with a lot of swear words, insisted that he didn't know Him. It didn't matter that this was his closest friend on earth and, indeed, his teacher and master. Three times he denied Him!

Now, days later, perhaps he's thinking that his denial of Jesus is unforgivable. So, he gives up and goes back to what he knows—fishing. The story goes on how the disciples fished all night and caught nothing. Then a stranger on the shore told them to put their nets on the other side of the boat. When they did, they caught tons of fish! Peter realized the stranger was Jesus!

When Peter came to shore, Jesus fed him breakfast and reassured him that he had been forgiven, that he was still needed, and that God had a big place for him in the gospel work! Read the story in Luke 22:54-62 and John 21:1-19. It's really good!

Sometimes we can get like Peter and began to think we are unforgivable. We may look at what we've done and think we can never be forgiven. But like all the Adams, Eves, Pauls, Davids and Rahabs of the world, we'll find that we can never go beyond the reach of God's forgiveness!

Dear Lord, thank You for Your faithfulness and Your forgiveness. There's been so many times I've come to You, and every time You've been faithful to Your Word! Thank You so much!

– Milly Jackson

Daily Bible Reading Plan: Exodus 4-6

JANUARY 23

We Have This Hope...

"We have this hope as an anchor for the soul, firm and secure. It enters the inner sanctuary behind the curtain, where our forerunner, Jesus, has entered on our behalf." Hebrews 6:19-20 (NIV)

The human soul . . . my soul, your soul . . . is most precious to God Almighty in all His creation. He created the human soul in His likeness and image to live forever and ever, eternally! Jesus said, "What good is it for someone to gain the whole world, yet forfeit their soul?" (Mark 8:36, NIV). The word *forfeit* means "losing." The sober thought here is someone could lose their soul for eternity, apart from God's eternal Kingdom.

Some years ago, I was fowl hunting with two other individuals on the mouth of a river in James Bay's west coast. Our hunting spot was on a shoal called Long Point. It was a good hunting spot, but only if the water tide was out. But it was also risky because when the high-water tide comes in, it can cover the whole shoal, making it dangerous if you're not careful.

After our hunt we came back to where we anchored our boat and motor. To our surprise our boat and motor were anchored further out into the water because of the high-water tide coming in, and we were unable to get to them with our hip waders.

Fortunately, the anchor was still holding tight enough to the mud part of the ground to keep the boat from floating away from us. I removed some clothes to walk into the cold water waist deep and managed to reach the rope. I pulled the anchor out and pulled the boat safely to the shore. The anchor held, otherwise we would have been in a tragic situation.

Be careful. Pay attention to your soul. Make sure your soul is anchored safely to the other side where Jesus is, who alone is our Hope. "Yes, my soul, find rest in God; my hope comes from Him" (Psalm 62:5, NIV).

– Abraham Jolly

Daily Bible Reading Plan: Exodus 7-8; Matthew 15

JANUARY 24

Yesterday, Today, and Forever

"Jesus Christ is the same yesterday and today and forever."
Hebrews 13:8 (NIV)

The Bible says that God is the same yesterday, today and forever. How can you know Him? By getting into His Word. It talks about Him forgiving our sins as far as the east is from the west. They are gone forever! We sin because of our human nature. I'm not saying it's okay, but when we sin we need to go quickly to the Lord and ask for forgiveness. God's Word says that He is faithful to forgive our sins. He did that yesterday. He's doing it today, and He will continue to do it!

God's Word also talks about His love for us, even when we were so far from Him. He loved us then, He loves us now, and He will love us forever. His love is the same as the day we came to Him. He never changes . . . *we* do!

God also talks about His plan for our lives. I know we will hit bumps in the road. Sometimes we feel alone. Sometimes we feel He is not answering our prayers. Sometimes we get confused as to what He is doing in our lives. We must remember He just wants the best for us. He says that we give our children the best gifts we can give—how much more will God give!

How we live our lives is very important. We aren't like Him—we can't be the same yesterday and forever, but we can determine in our heart that we will serve the Lord every day. Take account of your life to see if you are still walking with and talking to Jesus. Do this often because one day we will stand before Him and give an account for how we have lived for Him while on this earth. Besides, we want others to see Him in us. We want to be true to Him . . . *always*!

– Pat Hall

Daily Bible Reading Plan: Exodus 9-11

JANUARY 25

Promises Kept

"As long as the earth endures, seedtime and harvest, cold and heat, summer and winter, day and night will never cease." Genesis 8:22 (NIV)

It was early September and as the first green tree morphed to yellow, the thought came to me, "Here we go again. Pretty soon the snow'll be flying!" In Cree we'd say, "Kiiyipa wii mispoon." No matter how you say it, there's no getting around the changing seasons!

The changing tree color brought to mind the passage in Genesis 8:22 of how the seasons came to be. It came out of God's promise made to Noah after the worldwide flood was over.

Well, that got me thinking about God's promises. When He gives us a promise, it's not a half-baked "maybe," but an absolute certainty!

Did you ever stop to think of how the seasons come about? Very simply, they are caused by the "tilt" of our planet that is spinning like a top as it circles the sun. That's the cold hard science behind our annual seasons and "cold weather coming."

This postdiluvian (after the biblical Flood) promise about the seasons would have involved God putting His hand on our planet and tipping the axis of the earth to create what we now know as seasons. That's awesome!

It's just so good to know that our Creator keeps His promises!

– Kene Jackson

Daily Bible Reading Plan: Exodus 12-13; Matthew 16

JANUARY 26

My Grace is All You Need

"My grace is all you need. My power works best in weakness. So now I am glad to boast about my weaknesses, so that the power of Christ can work through me." 2 Corinthians 12:9 (NLT)

The apostle Paul was given a "thorn in the flesh." Some scholars believe it had to do with his eyesight. Whatever the case, Paul prayed that God would take it away. However, God did not take it away. Why? God had allowed Paul to see amazing visions and revelations (vs. 2)—definitely something to boast about! Yet God says to Paul, "My power works best in weakness."

Paul was not complaining after that. Instead, he said he is glad when he is weak, insulted, going through hardships, persecutions, and troubles. Even when suffering for Christ, he can say this because it was not his own strength, but Christ's strength in him. Although we can't boast about things like Paul, there are times when we can find ourselves in "boasting mode"—not realizing that it is God who helps us.

When I became a follower of Jesus, I knew that someday I would have to share my testimony with people. I was painfully shy. Well, God sure had a sense of humor when He called me and showed that He is able to use even me, this shy girl.

Yet I needed to be willing to be used for God. So, I surrendered my shyness over to God and was willing to speak and share my testimony to many people about how He has forgiven me and given me new life in Him. To the world's standards I was weak to start with, but He saw His child willing to step out of her comfort zone to share about Him. Now He has also given me opportunities to teach the Bible! What greater way to be used by Him—by His strength and marvelous grace!

– Myrna Kopf

Daily Bible Reading Plan: Exodus 14-15; Matthew 17

JANUARY 27

Neutral is Not an Option

"Choose for yourselves this day whom you will serve . . . but as for me and my house, we will serve the Lord." Joshua 24:15 (NKJV)

"Each one hopes that if he feeds the crocodile enough, the crocodile will eat him last. All of them hope that the storm will pass before their turn comes to be devoured. But I fear—I fear greatly—the storm will not pass. It will rage and it will roar, even more loudly, even more widely," wrote Winston Churchill.

During the outbreak of World War 2 there were countries that chose to be neutral to the onslaught of the Nazis' invasions, in hopes of maintaining peace. But Churchill knew that closing their eyes to danger doesn't make it go away. It, in fact, emboldens the enemy.

Every day we are reminded how unbelievably chaotic our world is. And things once thought wrong are now acceptable. When we think bad is not that bad, we are in trouble. That kind of sentiment is sure to mislead us into believing all is good . . . or at least in the end will work itself out.

Turning a blind eye to works of the enemy is a poor approach to dealing with such a dangerous foe. For our enemy, that "food for thought" turns into a feast, and our enemy has an insatiable appetite that will not be satisfied.

If we believe we can maneuver through life without getting attacked by our enemy, we are sadly mistaken. If we believe we can deceive our enemy into believing we are no threat, we are deceived. Our enemy is like a roaring lion seeking whom he may devour (1 Peter 5:8). He does not play favorites. To remain neutral is not an option.

It is essential we make a choice about who we will serve. "Christ is either Lord of all, or He is not Lord at all," wrote James Hudson Taylor. "Our choice, our decision . . . every man is free to choose it or sadly refuse it."

– Rose Buck

Daily Bible Reading Plan: Exodus 16-18

JANUARY 28

A Life That Counts

"For the Son of man has come to seek and to save that which was lost." Luke 19:10 (NASB)

I never thought my life was worth much while growing up in the community where I lived. It seemed that I was the only one who would never amount to anything. Those days were lonely and frustrating, as many of the other kids would make fun of me.

"Why are they doing it?" I wondered. To this day, I don't know why they did that to me. It made me feel so alone.

As I look at Scripture and read about the people who Jesus chose, today I can look back and see how Jesus had me in His mind long before I was even born. He probably said, "Here is one I can use."

And He knew who I was. It's not that I am someone perfect or special, but Jesus can use anyone He chooses. If I was Jesus, I would never pick me, but He came to save and seek the lost, so I fit in that category. One day I knelt down and gave my life to Him.

Zacchaeus in the New Testament was despised by the people in his time. He was even hated, but Jesus chose him and used him. Zacchaeus gave his life to the Lord, and he was used by the Lord. You can read about him in the Bible in Luke 19.

Have you ever considered how God is willing to meet you right where you are? All He wants you to do is admit your need for Him. You, too, can come to Him by accepting His gift of salvation.

Father in Heaven, I feel so alone. But when I read in Luke 19, I read that Your Son, Jesus Christ, came to seek and save the lost. I don't want to be lost. I want to be found. I need You. I believe in You. I give my life to You.

– Liz Genaille

Daily Bible Reading Plan: Exodus 19-20; Matthew 18

JANUARY 29

A Call to Healing

"He heals the brokenhearted and binds up their wounds." Psalm 147:3 (NKJV)

In 2017 God was calling me to leave my husband, family, and home for three weeks to do security work nine hours away. Also, it was time to do some personal work on myself with God. I called it a "paid retreat"—where I learned to trust God and listen to His loving voice.

In the past I experienced mental, emotional, physical, and spiritual abuse at the Kamloops Indian Residential School. Trusting others didn't come easy. While away, during the pitch-black dark nights of the far north, I talked with God and asked why it still hurts so much from when my dad left in 2005. Can you envision a child lost and broken without her daddy? That was me.

As I talked to God, tears would roll down my cheeks. Soon they wouldn't stop. They were like steadily flowing streams. I shared with God how much I missed my dad. When I spoke about my dad, my throat got hoarse and tightened. My body trembled, and the tears rolled down my cheeks like a waterfall that would plunge over the bank.

I was wailing and telling God, "It's stuck in my throat. Get it out. I want it out!" I was sobbing uncontrollably. It took many conversations with God to be able to finally talk about my dad without crying. As I cried, He brought healing to my heart and spirit and, as I shared with Him, He reminded me of who I am in Him.

Heavenly Father, please guide me into a place of healing. Show me what issues I need to work on. Lord, let my weakness be your strength, let my pain be victory for your cause. I want to follow Your lead and be freed from the chains that hold me back from You.

– Jennifer McEwan

Daily Bible Reading Plan: Exodus 21-22; Matthew 19

JANUARY 30

Linked and Synced

"The eye cannot say to the hand, 'I don't need you!' And the head cannot say to the feet, 'I don't need you!'" . . . "But God has put the body together, giving greater honor to the parts that lacked it, so that there should be no division in the body, but that its parts should have equal concern for each other. If one part suffers, every part suffers with it; if one part is honored, every part rejoices with it." 1 Corinthians 12:21, 24-26 (NIV)

We are just getting through a technical electronics issue at our place. A friend thought it would be a great idea to "link and sync" all our electronics . . . so we let her! It didn't take too long to figure out that it may not be that good a concept.

Now, every time a FaceTime call comes in, both our iPads and both iPhones start ringing at the same time (all with different rings)! It sounds like 11 cats scrapping it out in the feline division of WWF's Battle Royal! Even if I'm 100 miles away, I pick up my wife's calls, and vice versa. We'll be "de-linking and de-syncing" very soon. This is just not working!

But meanwhile, it kind of reminds me of the description of God's family in 1 Corinthians 12. We see there that we are all linked as family and, when one member is hurting, everyone hurts. When one is celebrating, the others celebrate with them. That's because we are one as a family. I hurt for my brother, and they do the same for me when I'm the hurting unit.

God put things together that way and, in His Family, it works! (It just doesn't translate when it comes to electronics!)

– Kene Jackson

Daily Bible Reading Plan: Exodus 23-24; Matthew 20

JANUARY 31

I Ate a Bug

"A friend loveth at all times." Proverbs 17:17a (KJV)

I ate a bug . . . not just any bug, I ate a roach.

My friend, Francis, was sweet and painfully shy. She worked as a bank teller 20 years and she lived with her parents until she was in her forties. At last Francis got the courage to leave home and get her own apartment. Francis decided to have her first party in her new apartment and invited her closest friends.

She'd worked hard to have everything perfect, and she'd cooked all the food herself. I sat next to Francis, and she filled a bowl with her homemade soup and set it in front of me. I scooped up some soup in my spoon and, just before I got it to my mouth, I saw a dead roach floating in the soup.

I looked up to see Francis smiling happily at me, waiting for me to taste her special soup. I looked around the table—everyone was watching me. I couldn't say, "Oh, there's a roach in my soup." If I put my spoon back into the bowl someone else might see the roach floating around. If Francis knew there was a roach in the soup, she'd be humiliated and probably never have another party in her life. I couldn't embarrass her. I smiled at Francis, opened my mouth, and swallowed the soup . . . and the roach.

Everyone had a wonderful time; the food was delicious; Francis was thrilled her first party was a success. Every few months, Francis would invite her friends for a special dinner, and I never missed one of them. Francis is loved by her family, her co-workers, and her friends.

I need to let Francis be Francis because that is what she does best, and I like her just the way she is. I like her so much, I'd eat a bug.

Thank you, God, for friends.

– Crying Wind

Daily Bible Reading Plan: Exodus 25-26

FEBRUARY 1

The Importance of Godly Parenting

"Choose you this day whom ye will serve . . ." Joshua 24:15a (KJV)

This scripture was forever ingrained in my mind as a young child. Growing up in our home a plaque hung on our living room wall with the above Bible scripture. "Choose ye this day whom you will serve," it said.

I was blessed with Christian parents who modeled the verse for us. Our late mother was the first to accept the Lord in her heart, and life at home forever changed. From that point on our home had Christian material, and church became a part of life. Even though I was exposed to religion all my life, it was mandatory that we attend church once a week, as encouraged by our late father.

It was from that background I found myself attending a revival service one Sunday evening at our community hall. The evangelist shared a salvation message and made an altar call.

I found myself at the front with at least 15 other young people who had responded. We were convicted of our sins, repented, and it was that evening God revealed his Son Jesus Christ as my Lord and Savior. It was the beginning of my spiritual journey.

The main point I am making is the importance for parents/homes to create an environment where children/loved ones are exposed to God's Word. You never know what it will do for young minds.

Hebrews 4:12 states, "For the word of God is quick and powerful, and sharper than any two-edged sword, piercing even to the dividing asunder of soul and spirit, and of the joints and marrow, and is a discerner of the thoughts and intents of the heart." (KJV)

– Liz Beardy

Daily Bible Reading Plan: Exodus 27-28; Matthew 21

FEBRUARY 2

Submission Brings Transformation

"So he went down and dipped himself seven times in the Jordan, according to the word of the man of God." 2 Kings 5:14a (ESV)

As a follower of Christ, I have found that life can be difficult and unexpected events can challenge our resolve in our pilgrimage. The unexpected storm of grief, death, pain, trauma, or abandonment in life can lead to a long, difficult, dry and discouraging wilderness season.

The storm seems to be invincible and hope of overcoming seeps from our hearts. Despite the trials that confront us, the Lord in abundant mercy and grace has given us spiritual gifts to help us endure these seasons.

The Word of God, prayer, and the comfort of the Holy Spirit empower us with spiritual endurance and strength to hang on with all steadfastness. Faithfully maintaining our devotional life during these times may decline and can become a practice of the joyous past.

Every follower of Christ knows this truth. Satan, our adversary of old, desires that dust will accumulate on our Bible and that our active prayer life discontinue.

Inevitably, this will diminish the comforting presence of the Holy Spirit, as the seeds of doubt and discouragement germinate and take residence. The enemy will attack us with the thought that maintaining a consistent devotional life is not the solution and is counterintuitive.

However, instead of throwing in the proverbial towel, the secret to enduring is to submit, yield, and remain obedient to the Word of God despite the ongoing trial. You can read more about this tomorrow.

– Steve Keesic

Daily Bible Reading Plan: Exodus 29-30

FEBRUARY 3

Submission Brings Transformation (Part 2)

"So he went down and dipped himself seven times in the Jordan, according to the word of the man of God, and his flesh was restored like the flesh of a little child, and he was clean." 2 Kings 5:14 (ESV)

Yesterday I mentioned how the Word of God, prayer, and the comfort of the Holy Spirit empower us with spiritual endurance and strength to hang on with all steadfastness. Faithfully maintaining our devotional life during these times may decline and can become a practice of the joyous past.

To help us understand this, let's consider Naaman, a great honorable mighty man of valor and captain in the army of the King of Syria. Despite his significant status in the kingdom, he suffered tremendously as a leper. Certainly, afflicted with physical pain, but undoubtedly tormented with thoughts of hopelessness and despair daily.

Scripture tells us that the remedy the Lord offered to Naaman (through his prophet Elisha) was to "dip" himself seven times in the Jordan River.

Initially, Naaman was angry and dismissed washing in the Jordan River as foolishness. However, once Naaman submitted, yielded and obeyed the Word of the Lord, his life was totally transformed! Can you imagine the great joy that Naaman experienced once he realized that leprosy had left him? The solution was the very action that he had recently dismissed!

Friend, your season of discouragement is coming to an end. Continue to submit, yield and obey the Word of God and your life will be transformed!

Ask yourself: "Holy Spirit, is there anything in my life that I need to submit to the Lord?"

Lord Jesus, remind me to spend time in Your Word and prayer each day. Help me to be faithful in this difficult season of life and trust that Your love will transform my situation.

– Steve Keesic

Daily Bible Reading Plan: Exodus 31-33

FEBRUARY 4

Wrong Way

"Jesus answered, 'I am the way and the truth and the life. No one comes to the Father except through me.'" John 14:6 (NIV)

Cain was the first one who tried it. Multitudes have emulated him over the years, and it's become a popular theme in today's post-Christian North American spiritual quagmire. Simply put, it is the concept that a person can come to God via some other way/bridge/road/belief or approach than what God has mapped out for us.

The story in Genesis 4 tells how Cain thought he could replace the required blood sacrifice with the fruit, veggies, and grains that he had grown. The desired outcome of spiritual cleansing (forgiveness of sin) should be available no matter what methodology was used . . . right?

Nope! He was wrong, just like every copycat since then. God had outlined to that first family how they were to approach Him, but Cain thought he could do it his way. And, like those who try today, he failed miserably with that approach.

We also have been given the God-given and God-approved way to reach Him. John 14:6 says that Jesus is the Way, the Truth and the Life, and that no one can approach or access Him by any other means. There is no shortcut or "secondary GPS routing"—just Jesus.

Let's keep Jesus at the center of our message and ministry.

– Kene Jackson

Daily Bible Reading Plan: Exodus 34-35; Matthew 22

FEBRUARY 5

Residential School

"Children are a gift from the Lord, they are a reward from him." Psalm 127:3 (NLT)

As a child, I remember going for a ride with my parents and siblings one day after sundown. My dad was trying to convince my mom to send us to residential school, since our family was growing so fast, and he wanted to save mom from having too much work.

I remember Mom saying, "No, I will never send my kids there. Those people don't know who God is!" She convinced Dad that this was not a solution. Dad believed in God, too, but didn't go to church (though he had been raised going to church). Once again, Mom strengthened my faith in Jesus just by standing her ground to keep us from potential harm at the residential school.

She never spoke of her own experience in the residential school but was very sure she did not want us girls to go there. It wasn't until I met and married the father of my children that I started to hear the terrible things that happened in residential school—the very poor conditions. He spoke of having to steal apples from the orchard due to hunger, and children who tried to escape being brought back and punished in front of everyone. The abuses were many from these people who claimed to represent God.

It is miraculous how some people who suffered these abuses came to believe in Jesus and accepted Him as their Lord and Savior! As it says in Jeremiah 29:11, " 'For I know the plans I have for you,' declares the Lord, 'plans to prosper you and not to harm you, plans to give you a hope and a future.' " (NIV) The man I married did just that, and trusted Jesus, amazed at God's love for him.

Dear Heavenly Father, thank You for Your plan for our lives. Thank You for Your Son Jesus, and the Holy Spirit who seals us as Yours.

– Loretta Oppenheim

Daily Bible Reading Plan: Exodus 36-38

FEBRUARY 6

Guiding Arcturus

"Canst thou guide Arcturus with his sons?" Job 38:32b (KJV)

I felt like I had missed something. I needed to go back to the library and find the astronomy book again. I had researched the star groupings of Pleiades and Orion that God had pointed out to Job (in Job 38:31), but I had no idea what I had missed. I thumbed through pages, searching chapter headings. Then I saw it: Arcturus.

We can find Arcturus by locating the first bright star off the handle of the Big Dipper. Arcturus (also called "the Bear" in the NIV) is 23 times the size of our sun (we can fit nearly a million earths into our sun), and it is 37 light years away. The most amazing fact is that it is one of the fastest moving stars in our Milky Way galaxy and was headed straight for our planetary system! This would not be good; yet, over the years, its forward speed slowed and its sideways speed picked up, causing it to miss us.

Have you ever felt like your life was out of control? Job went through great loss as Satan plotted to cause him to curse God to His face. God even allowed Satan to touch Job's body with suffering. Satan wanted God to know that no person would ever simply love Him for Himself, but only for what humanity could get from Him.

After God revealed Himself through His creation, Job said, "My ears had heard of you, but now my eyes have seen you" (Job 42:5, NIV). God, in all of His magnificence and power, loved Job. He hoped Job would love Him back, even when things were difficult. As we look at what God made, we can ask ourselves: is He worthy of our love?

Lord, open my eyes so I can see who You really are. I want to love You no matter what—not because of what You give me, but because You are You.

– Sue Carlisle

Daily Bible Reading Plan: Exodus 39-40; Matthew 23

FEBRUARY 7

The Power of God's Word

"In the beginning God created the heaven and the earth. And God said, 'Let there be light: and there was light.'" Genesis 1:1-3 (KJV)

I am not sure how much I can grasp the power of God's Word as in the above Scripture. With one word Almighty God created the heaven and earth to existence. With one word, there was light. Let that sink in a bit. We serve a powerful and amazing God! Throughout the Bible, here is how He displayed His power:

The parting of the Red Sea to bring His people out of bondage (Exodus 14) . . . Jericho's walls fell as the Israelites marched around the city (Joshua 6) . . . God saved Daniel in the lions' den (Daniel 6) . . . Elijah was lifted to heaven on chariots of fire (2 Kings 2) . . . The birth of the Messiah, Jesus Christ (Matthew 2) . . . Lazarus raised from the dead (John 11) . . . Jesus died to save us from our sins (John 3) . . . God raised Jesus from the dead (Romans 6) . . . Jesus ascended back to heaven, and in the same way will return (Luke 24).

These are just a few examples—you may have your own favorite Bible stories about God's power that have impacted you. Hebrews 4:12 says: "For the word of God is quick (living), and powerful, and sharper than any two-edged sword, piercing even to the dividing asunder of soul and spirit, and of the joints and marrow, and is a discerner (able to judge) of the thoughts and intents of the heart." (KJV, clarification added)

I often mention, when counseling, that my own words are so limited. But when we apply God's Word, it goes way deeper into our hearts and can bring us out of bondage. It is so important to meditate on His Word each day. David said in Psalm 119:11: "Thy word have I hid in my heart that I may not sin against thee." (KJV) I pray God will give each of us a greater desire to understand His Word.

– Liz Beardy

Daily Bible Reading Plan: Leviticus 1-3

FEBRUARY 8

God Cares About the Little Things

"Give all your worries and cares to God, for he cares about you."
1 Peter 5:7 (NLT)

God blessed me with the opportunity to attend Briercrest Bible College, which I am very thankful for. During my time at Briercrest, I was part of the College Singers and loved every minute of it. Each Christmas, Briercrest put on a huge production and had multiple presentations, which we started practicing for weeks beforehand.

I have such great memories of being a part of those concerts. Singing as a group with all the intricate harmonies and parts deepened my love for music and was one way I worshiped and felt closer to God.

In December 2020, fifteen years after I graduated, I was telling my mom how much I missed being a part of College Singers. It was a quiet desire of my heart. About a week later I received an email from Briercrest saying they wanted to do a video of "Agnus Dei" and invited me to record singing the alto harmony. What a blessing! I was nervous at first because I hadn't sung in so long but, with some encouragement, I decided to go for it. (They compiled all the video submissions and created a virtual choir that year.)

God cares about the big *and* little things—the desires and the disappointments and worries. Just give them to God. Oh, how wonderful God is! How He cares about and loves us.

Thank you, Father, for knowing exactly what we need before we ask. You are a mighty God who still cares about the little things in our heart.

– Leana Patenaude

Daily Bible Reading Plan: Leviticus 4-5; Matthew 24

FEBRUARY 9

Heaven Can Wait

"You have turned my mourning into dancing." Psalm 30:11 (KJV)

We all want to go to Heaven. But not yet ... not now. Last year I had a minor heart attack. I went to a doctor and I asked him, "Am I going to die?" He laughed and said, "We're *all* going to die!" That wasn't the answer I wanted or expected, and I resented his laughter.

Okay, it's true that everyone dies, and everything dies, but we all want it to be in the distant future ... not now. Even "good Christians" who are looking forward to Heaven, are not in a hurry to die. There are things they want to do, places they want to go, people they want to see.

The Bible mentions heaven hundreds of times. We want to go there ... but not now. We have today, and maybe tomorrow, and maybe a few years or more. What are we going to do with the time we have left? I cleaned house, threw away bags of clothes, papers, "stuff" and clutter I didn't want to leave behind for my children to dispose of. I planned my funeral.

I received a large box from my best friend. When I opened the box, there was a big stuffed toy cow that played music and danced and flipped into the air and did somersaults and mooed. As it flipped across my kitchen floor, I started to laugh for the first time in months. I was laughing so hard, tears of joy were running down my face. I couldn't remember the last time I'd laughed so much.

I wasn't dead yet. I was alive. I might live for years, yet I was preparing for my death and funeral and not wasting whatever time I had left. I was alive and apparently, I needed a musical cow bouncing around my kitchen to remind me I was alive and could still laugh.

Lord, I'm looking forward to Heaven ... but not yet.

– Crying Wind

Daily Bible Reading Plan: Leviticus 6-7; Matthew 25

FEBRUARY 10

Broken Strings

"It is for freedom that Christ has set us free. Stand firm, then, and do not let yourselves be burdened again by a yoke of slavery."
Galatians 5:1 (NIV)

Just before we left on a tour to Alaska, I bought some cheap bass guitar strings. Figuring that they'd do for the trip, I saved a few bucks and wound them onto my Fender Precision. We were only three days in when the first one broke! I didn't think too much about it until the second one snapped a week later. Then the third! Before that last "E" string followed the doomed path of its predecessors, I preemptively changed it! Since there was no place to buy new ones, I finished the tour on "recycled" strings.

The problem with broken strings is that they throw everything out of tune! All the other strings change pitch when one breaks. It sounds horrible and you need to change that wire ASAP.

When we allow sinful things in our lives, they have the same effect as a broken guitar string—throwing our spiritual lives out of whack. When things like unforgiveness, envy, bitterness, self-pity, or selfishness are allowed to creep in and hang around and get a foothold in our soul, our whole spiritual "melody" goes sour.

We find that it becomes hard to pray, that our attitude gets stale and moldy, and "Joy" is just the long-forgotten name of our third-grade teacher! . . . until you change that broken string. Whatever it takes to deal with your spiritual disharmony, get it done! Give forgiveness. Work on the attitude. Let go of the self-pity. Dump the bitterness and let God replace your selfishness with His ways. It's only when you get rid of that dysfunctional string that your spiritual melody can become sweet and real.

– Kene Jackson

Daily Bible Reading Plan: Leviticus 8-10

FEBRUARY 11

Spiritual Breath

"If we say that we have fellowship with Him and yet walk in the darkness, we lie and do not practice the truth; but if we walk in the light as He Himself is in the light, we have fellowship with one another, and the blood of Jesus His Son cleanses us from all sin."
1 John 1:6,7 (NASB)

As a young Christian, I attended a seminar given by Bill Bright of Campus Crusade for Christ. I learned about a process called spiritual breathing. This practice has kept me in touch with God to this day.

Put simply, spiritual breathing means to confess our sins, which is exhaling, and asking the Holy Spirit to take control and guide us, which is inhaling.

1 John 1:9 (NIV) says, "If we confess our sins, He is faithful and just and will forgive us our sins and purify us from all unrighteousness." In addition, in Ephesians 5:18 (AMP) God instructs us: "Be filled with the [Holy] Spirit *and* constantly guided by Him."

I believe that this is extremely important in our walk with God. To receive ready answers to prayer and continued growth in our faith, we must keep the flow of the Spirit in our lives. Romans chapter 7 expresses how, as human beings, we constantly battle with our lower natures. Then chapter 8 of Romans relates the victory we can have as we walk in the Spirit.

In my journey, I have learned that spiritual breathing is essential for me to please God and serve Him unimpeded.

God in heaven, have mercy on us and help us in our weaknesses. Help us to remember that You are waiting to help us to triumph over our lower nature and walk in the power of the Holy Spirit.

– Theresa Bose

Daily Bible Reading Plan: Leviticus 11-12

FEBRUARY 12

Why They See Jesus in Us

"For you were formerly darkness, but now you are a light in the Lord; walk as children of light." Ephesians 5:7 (NASB)

Just because I am a born-again Christian does not mean I don't have struggles. One that I remember clearly was when a young teenage boy had beaten up one of our sons in school with a hard object. He hurt him pretty bad. As a mother this was hard to take, but God gave me grace to forgive.

Not long after this had happened, the young teen came to our home and asked for my son. At the time, I was having a bad day and was tired. I grumbled at him and said, "What do you want here? He's not home. Go away!" So, the teen went away.

A few minutes later God's Holy Spirit spoke to my heart about my attitude and rude words. I felt convicted and felt so awful. I told my husband, Bert, to pray with me. We prayed for this young teen, that there would be another opportunity to talk to him. A few days later he came back and, thank God, our prayer was answered!

This is the conversation that he and I had. I said, "I was really mad at you for what you did. That's why I even laid charges against you. But I dropped the charges, as God would not let me do that, and this is the reason why.

"I read in the Bible how people beat up Jesus Christ, God's own Son, and God forgave those people. So now I want to tell you that I forgive you for what you did to my son. I am sorry for being rude to you. Will you also forgive me? I am a Christian and I love Jesus. Now I want to tell you that Jesus loves you and wants to be your friend, so you can have everlasting life in Heaven with Him, if you give your life to Him."

– Liz Genaille

Daily Bible Reading Plan: Leviticus 13; Matthew 26

FEBRUARY 13

Praying for Our Kids

"Do not be anxious about anything, but in every situation, by prayer and petition, with thanksgiving, present your requests to God."
Philippians 4:6 (NIV)

Did you ever wake up at night and couldn't go back to sleep? You tossed and turned, but sleep wouldn't come. Sometimes when that happens, I realize that I can make good use of that time, so I start to pray.

Usually, the first ones that come to mind are my kids. I wonder where they're at, and I pray about that. I wonder how they're doing, and I pray about that. I wonder if they need God's guidance, and I pray about that. I wonder if they can sense that I'm praying for them.

I pray about other things: friends, situations, health issues, and whatever else comes to mind at three o'clock in the morning. But most of all I pray for my kids and grandkids!

Sometimes we get concerned about the direction our kids are taking (sometimes it's the grandkids), decisions they're making, and where God fits into their lives. We can bring all that to the Lord, and I let them know that sometimes they get extra prayers in the middle of the night!

Don't waste your midnight sleeplessness. Use that time to pray!

Dear God, thank You for the power of prayer. Thank You that I can always trust You to take care of my children, grandchildren, and those I care about. Amen.

– Milly Jackson

Daily Bible Reading Plan: Leviticus 14

FEBRUARY 14

When You Doubt God's Forgiveness

"The sacrifices of God are a broken spirit, a broken and a contrite heart—these, O God, You will not despise." Psalm 51:17 (NKJV)

Whether you were saved at age 12, or accepted Christ as your Savior as an adult, you may have sinned many times since then. Your sins may be so terrible that they lead you to despair and cause you to believe that there is no way God will ever forgive you. You may wonder if you are still saved. But what does Scripture say about God's forgiveness?

The disciple Peter asked Jesus to call to him as He walked on water. For a short time, Peter walks toward Jesus on the water. Peter later denied three times that he even knew Jesus. After Jesus was resurrected from the dead, the disciple Thomas denied that the resurrection had even taken place, although Jesus had promised them that He would be raised up on the third day. Then Jesus spent 40 days with them after His resurrection.

Another example of God's abiding love and promised forgiveness is King David's sin with Bathsheba, the wife of loyal and trusting Uriah. To cover his transgression, David orchestrated Uriah's death. Yet, God not only forgave David, He even allowed him to remain king. God forgives us our sins if we repent, but He may also sternly discipline us.

The wonderful gift of God is that when we repent, He also forgets our sins (Jeremiah 31:34) and reassures us that "As far as the east is from the west, so far has He removed our transgressions from us" (Psalms 103:12, NKJV).

Our Father in heaven, in the name of Jesus, help us to place our complete trust in Your promise that whatsoever we ask in prayer, believing, we shall have.

– Kiki BelMonte-Schaller

Daily Bible Reading Plan: Leviticus 15-16

FEBRUARY 15

Carried by the Wind

"That we should no longer be children, tossed to and fro and carried about with every wind of doctrine." Ephesians 4:14 (NKJV)

An Inuit man told me how he and his friend, while they were fishing, suddenly found themselves adrift on ice. The ice had broken off closer to land. Early in the winter the ice on Hudson Bay does not cover the whole area. It breaks up with the wind and then freezes again. The ice surface is very rough.

These two men were fishing when they noticed that they were slowly drifting away from land. They rushed back, but the crack was already too wide to cross. For a day and a night, they drifted out to sea. Then by the mercy of God the wind shifted and brought them back to land.

The Bible tells us to grow spiritually into maturity and not to be "carried about with every wind of doctrine." Like these men on the ice who had to go whichever direction the wind was blowing, believers who are not going by the Word of God are also carried about by all kinds of teaching and experiences that are not in line with God's Word. Sometimes teachings from the Bible are twisted to fit into the wrong thinking of a person.

God wants us to take His Word as the source from which we get guidance in our Christian walk. If we ask, the Holy Spirit will give us understanding as we read God's Word.

We should ask ourselves, am I getting my directions from God through His Word or am I listening to everyone who comes along? Am I allowing the Holy Spirit to be my teacher?

Dear Lord, I pray that You will give me understanding and direction from Thy Word.

– Bill Jackson

Daily Bible Reading Plan: Leviticus 17-18; Matthew 27

FEBRUARY 16

Wait Upon the Lord

"He gives power to the faint; and to them that have no might he increases strength. Even the youths shall faint and be weary, and the young men shall utterly fall: But they that wait upon the Lord shall renew their strength, they shall mount up with wings as eagles; they shall run, and not be weary; and they shall walk and not faint." Isaiah 40:29-31 (KJV)

I have been recently meditating on this scripture, especially as I look around and see the increase of sin and death. People are dying and losing heart from all the losses we face today.

I work as a Christian mental health counselor, and I am touched many times as I listen to those who seek help. I am especially touched by the youth who have lost hope and have no sense of belonging anywhere. Sadly, our communities are filled with broken homes and families.

This scripture takes me back to one of the greatest prophets from the Old Testament. Isaiah wrote, "Even the youths shall faint and be weary and the young men shall utterly fall." I take to heart what he prophesied has become our reality. Are young men losing heart and utterly falling?

I work in an area where there is a high suicide rate among young people, and many of us grasp at what would help. Isaiah wrote, "But they that wait upon the Lord shall renew their strength." In the Hebrew language, "wait" means hopeful anticipation, submission to the Lord's will, and trusting in the Lord.

Believers in Christ have the answer that "Jesus is the way the truth and the life" (John 14:6). Let us keep sharing the gospel of Jesus Christ to the lost and hurting. Pray for our youth to find Jesus and to experience what Isaiah wrote . . . "They shall mount up with wings as eagles; they shall run, and not be weary; and they shall walk and not faint."

– Liz Beardy

Daily Bible Reading Plan: Leviticus 19-20

FEBRUARY 17

Free Boosting!

"Jesus himself said: 'It is more blessed to give than to receive.'"
Acts 20:35b (NIV)

Christmas had always been a time for me to "get" things. Right from my first memories of toy trucks under the tree, it's been that way. I remember the Christmas when I decided to do it different . . .

In Canada we have Kijiji (it's like Craigslist), where I posted an ad: "Free Boosting. Anytime, anywhere around Calgary. Just call me! Merry Christmas!" I added a picture of some booster cables, gassed up the old Jeep 4x4, and started to field the calls that came in.

It was really cold and snowy when I started, about the 10th of December. Some days there would be only one call, but some days there'd be four or five. Some calls came at about 9:00 o'clock at night, and I'd go out in the dark to get them started. Some chipped in for gas and some didn't. Someone even saved my number and called me six months later for a boost!

I kept going until December 23rd when I pulled the ad off and allowed AAA to regain their market share!

It really made a difference in my "Yuletide attitude"! I got way more excited about what I was doing for others than what was in it for me. And when the total stranger I was helping asked how come I was doing this, I'd get the chance to tell them that Jesus had given me so much in life, I was just trying to give a little back!

– Kene Jackson

Daily Bible Reading Plan: Leviticus 21-22; Matthew 28

FEBRUARY 18

To Future Generations

"Therefore, let us not grow weary of doing good, for in due season we will reap, if we do not give up." Galatians 6:9 (ESV)

"The greatest legacy one can pass onto one's children and grandchildren is not money or other material things accumulated in one's life, but rather a legacy of character and faith," wrote Billy Graham.

Growing up, every Sunday my father would tackle the old familiar obstacle course of getting us up and ready for church. They say, "Each day has enough trouble of its own," and I'm certain we doubled the task for dad those particular mornings!

But he never gave up on us. When Sunday came along, all of us knew we were going to church whether we wanted to or not. It was something that my dad wanted for us as children in his family—to be able to attend church together. It was difficult because we didn't want to go.

As an adult, I appreciate the work that it took to persuade us to go to church. It's a memory that I cherish to know that my father and mother's concern for us was not only our physical care, but our spiritual well-being. I am thankful for a home that saw God as being a part of who we were and realizing that without Him we would flounder.

Future generations depend on it. Don't give up. It may seem like a daunting task in this day and age, but it is not impossible. Our hope is to trust God and leave the outcome to Him.

Lord, we pray that the spiritual truths we learn will continue to pass on to future generations. We pray the lives of our children may hold fast to the Word of God, that it is being embedded securely in their hearts, and they may find life abundantly.

– Rose Buck

Daily Bible Reading Plan: Leviticus 23-24

FEBRUARY 19

Is Your Anchor Holding?

"We have this hope as an anchor for the soul, firm and secure. It enters the inner sanctuary behind the curtain." Hebrews 6:19 (NIV)

Several years ago, I worked on a packer boat. We transferred west coast salmon from fish collectors to the cannery. In the bay one day the captain gave orders to lower the ship's anchor. Down went the anchor, then followed the chain, and then the cable. The anchor picked up speed, so the captain said to apply the brake to slow it down, but the brake failed. Down went the anchor, picking up speed. Then, to our surprise, the end of the cable disappeared from sight! The cable was not secured. We lost the anchor, chain, and cable. We had to head back to the dock—a ship must have an anchor. That anchor still lies on the bottom of the ocean 54 years later.

God cannot lie when He says something. This is a great help to us who have come to God for safety. It encourages us to hold on to the hope that is ours. This hope is like an anchor, strong and keeping us safe. It goes behind the curtain. Jesus has already entered there and opened the way for us. He has become our high priest forever (Hebrews 6), interceding for us.

Jesus is our hope and anchor and will keep us in the midst of life's storms. Unlike a ship's anchor, His anchor will not fail. A time will come when He will call all believers to that blessed place He has prepared for us, a time will come when all our storms will cease. For now, when trouble comes, we must be steadfast in the faith and trust God.

If you have never accepted Jesus Christ as Lord and Savior, be encouraged to do it right now. Knowing Jesus as Lord is the true remedy for peace in the midst of your storm.

– Terry Hall

Daily Bible Reading Plan: Leviticus 25; Mark 1

FEBRUARY 20

No Condemnation

"So now there is no condemnation for those who belong to Christ Jesus. And because you belong to Him, the power of the life-giving Spirit has freed you from the power of sin that leads to death."
Romans 8:1-2 (NLT)

These verses are meaningful to me as a follower of Christ because, when I sin, not only does Jesus forgive me when I ask Him, but I also belong to Him! Although this does not give me permission to keep on deliberately sinning, He has freed me from the power of sin because of His Spirit in me. His Spirit causes me to be convicted of sin and aware of what is wrong and what is right.

There was a time I remember, just a few days after I asked Jesus to forgive me of my sins and make me clean, that I became more aware of my choice of words. At school, my combination lock was not reading my numbers—or was I just mixing them up? I was late for class and getting impatient. Next thing I knew, I swore.

Wow, I felt and knew that this wasn't a word I should be using. I wouldn't have cared before, but I just didn't feel right in continuing to use this offensive language.

In all honesty, there are times that I fail and continue to sin. But immediately I confess it and ask God to forgive me. At times guilt has still hovered over me, and I kept asking God to forgive me. Usually, Satan will try to keep us from trusting that God has the power to forgive our sin. Then I came upon this verse in Romans 8:1, and how liberating it was to read it! "So now there is no condemnation for those who belong to Christ Jesus."

As a child of God, there is no condemnation—I have been forgiven!

– Myrna Kopf

Daily Bible Reading Plan: Leviticus 26-27; Mark 2

FEBRUARY 21

Edgar the Crow

"Let birds fly ... across the vault of the sky." Genesis 1:20b (NIV)

One day when I was walking in the woods, I found a tiny baby bird hopping around in the grass. I gently picked him up and looked at the huge oak tree that appeared to have a bird's nest near the top. There was no way to get the baby bird back to its nest, so I took it home with me.

The bird was old enough to have black pin feathers and I thought it might be a raven, so I named him Edgar after Edgar Allen Poe. I bought a cage and toys and birdseed. He would sit on my finger and eat out of my hand. He would chirp when I came into the room.

I discovered he was not a raven—he was a crow, but I continued to call him "Edgar," after Mr. Poe's raven. On sunny days, I would carry his cage out to the patio so he could enjoy the sunshine and fresh air and the songs of the other birds.

He had more than tripled in size and was a full-grown crow now. One day when I went out to feed him, he was out of his cage—he had pushed the door on his cage open. He was sitting on the patio table. I put my hand out and he hopped onto my finger. I could put him back into the cage and keep him, but he needed to be with other birds. He needed his freedom, and he needed a mate.

"Goodbye, Edgar, it was nice knowing you," I said, and brushed him off my finger. He took flight and flew to the top of a pine tree. He hesitated only a few seconds and then flew away. I turned my back on him. I didn't want him to see the tears in my eyes.

Thank you, Lord, for all the wonderful creatures you made, especially birds who fly across the heavens like angels.

– Crying Wind

Daily Bible Reading Plan: Numbers 1-2; Mark 3

FEBRUARY 22

When Forgiveness Seems Too Hard

"And whenever you stand praying, if you have anything against anyone, forgive him, that your Father in heaven may also forgive you your trespasses." Mark 11:25 (NKJV)

She (we'll call her Sarah) and her friend Maya have been close chums since elementary school. They were more like sisters than friends. Then Sarah finds out that Maya has ditched her for a new crowd. Sarah is hurt. Angry. And vows to spread nasty rumors about her "friend" to avenge the betrayal!

Sarah's inner voice—which is the way God sometimes speaks to us—tells her to open her Bible. Sarah searches the concordance at the back of the Bible for the word "forgive." It takes her to Matthew 6:14, which says, "For if you forgive others their trespasses, your heavenly Father will also forgive you." (NKJV) Sarah quickly looks up the word "trespass" on her laptop. The antiquated definition means "to wrong somebody."

She keeps reading, then raises her eyes. "So, unless I forgive Maya, God won't forgive me, either. Besides, could there be some reason Maya is avoiding me?" Even the Lord's Prayer in Matthew 6:12 says, "And forgive us our debts as we also have forgiven our debtors. (NKJV)"

"Sounds like God won't forgive the unforgiver," she accepts with a sigh. "But I'll call Maya anyhow and chew her out first!" Just then her phone rings: "It's me, Maya. How about lunch tomorrow? My Oklahoma cousins are in town, and they're dying to meet you!"

"Cousins? Uh—sure," Sara agrees. After hanging up, tears cloud her eyes. "Thank you, Father God, for Maya's call. I would have done a terrible thing without even giving my closest friend a chance to explain!"

Gracious and loving Father God, thank You for Your goodness, forgiveness and grace through the Perfect Sacrifice, your precious Son, Jesus, in whose Name we pray. Amen.

– Kiki BelMonte-Schaller

Daily Bible Reading Plan: Numbers 3-4

FEBRUARY 23

Patience and Perseverance

"We who are powerful need to be patient with the weakness of those who don't have power, and not please ourselves." Romans 15:1 (CEB)

Moose hunting requires a hunter to be patient and to not be discouraged. It is about wind direction, body scent, camouflage, how to push a moose out of the bush and, most of all, have a careful aim.

Moose are very large animals and have very thick hides, so you need to ensure that if you are going to harvest a moose, you need to make sure that your kill shot is very accurate. But the most important thing in harvesting a moose is patience.

The Scripture verse above (Romans 15:1) reminds us to be patient with others. It would be easy to be patient if everyone did everything according to your plans. The true test God has given you is being patient with those who you find challenging.

Patience creates perseverance. We always want to get things done quickly, but we all know that when we start rushing anything in life, it never works. We are probably doing more damage in anything we are trying to achieve.

We know who is always in control and always has patience with us, and his name is Jesus. He is very powerful over everything to the weakness that we represent. If you want to learn patience, learn from the Teacher of patience.

He never gives up on us. He doesn't rush us to achieve what He feels is important to our lives. He would be a good moose hunting partner because He can teach us the skill of patience that we need daily in our lives. It is pleasing to Him to know that we use Him as our example to slow down when we are in a hurry trying to be successful. Patience is a virtue.

– Kirby James

Daily Bible Reading Plan: Numbers 5-6; Mark 4

FEBRUARY 24

Drive Safe!

"Let us throw off everything that hinders and the sin that so easily entangles, and let us run with perseverance the race marked out for us, fixing our eyes on Jesus." Hebrews 12:1b-2 (NIV)

I went for an eye exam the other day—my first time since 1994. I thought I should make sure that it was okay for me to drive without glasses. I guess it was, 'cuz I passed!

It got me to thinking about the conditions and stipulations we have on our driver's licenses. Ken Antone (of the Antone Indian Family singers) used to laugh about the "No food within reach" condition on his driver's license, saying "They just know me!"

Other conditions I've seen include prohibitions about night driving, TV in the driver's sight line, cell phone usage, seatbelts, medications, etc.—all intended to keep us focused on *driving safe.*

When it comes to our spiritual calling, we need to recognize that there are things that can distract and hinder us in that area also. If we allow them to, they'll bring us down. Whether it be poor financial decisions, COVID-19 pandemic over-focus, listening to bad advice, discouragement, unresolved grief or sinful choices, there are things that will derail us.

"Everything that hinders" can mean something different for each of us, but the end result is the same. If we let it go unchecked, it will drag us down. Hang in there and "drive safe!"

– Kene Jackson

Daily Bible Reading Plan: Numbers 7-8

FEBRUARY 25

I Have a Father

"So you have not received a spirit that makes you fearful slaves. Instead, you received God's Spirit when he adopted you as His own children. Now we call him, 'Abba, Father.'" Romans 8:15 (NLT)

In 2010, the opportunity arose for me to visit Israel and, of course, I jumped on that chance. My two aunties and cousin and I were ready to visit a place we had only read about in God's Word!

We were waking up one beautiful morning at a hotel near the Dead Sea and decided to go for breakfast. Although we were able to visit many neat locations that are mentioned in God's Word, for some reason what I heard that morning while having breakfast touched my heart.

As I was sitting with my family for breakfast, I overheard a young boy speak a word that I had only heard about in the Bible. I turned around and he was calling his dad. He said, "Abba!" The young boy was calling his dad! It touched my heart so deeply.

I grew up without a dad. When I was four years old, he was killed. How I longed to have a father. I never got to know what it was like to grow up with a dad and call him "Dad." When I see pictures of my dad, it is clear that I look a lot like him.

At 20 years of age, I put my faith in Jesus Christ and have followed Him since. I will be 50 years old this year. It is clear to me, as I have been learning, that even though I grew up without a father, that having put my faith in Jesus, I do have a father! . . . a heavenly Father! It is God, who I can call "Abba!" . . . which means "daddy" in Hebrew.

He is a Father who loves me unconditionally, totally, consistently—who will never leave me or forsake me. How beautiful it is to know Him.

– Myrna Kopf

Daily Bible Reading Plan: Numbers 9-11

FEBRUARY 26

Train Up a Child

"Train up a child in the way he should go; even when he is old he will not depart from it." Proverbs 22:6 (ESV)

I remember Deuteronomy 6:7 from the early years that my husband and I came to the Lord. It says, "You shall teach them diligently to your children, and shall talk of them when you sit in your house, when you walk by the way, when you lie down, when you rise up." (NKJV)

However, we were so busy being discipled and helping with the church planting of the Vancouver Native Fellowship that we failed to focus on teaching our own children as we were being taught. Children need to be taught, not left to their own devices. And more importantly, we need to reflect Jesus to them.

So, when I had the privilege of raising four of my grandchildren, we read the Bible with them every night (a Children's Bible). It had questions to answer at the end of each reading. It was a special time for all of us. As adults, my children and grandchildren have faith and believe in prayer.

It wasn't an easy task teaching our own children, even after dedicating them to the Lord. Things were moving so fast with both our lives in the Alcoholics Anonymous and Al-Anon programs, and the growing fellowship that began in our home and then at the Vancouver Indian Centre.

I will always be a strong advocate for teaching little children about Jesus, telling them how He came as a baby, grew into a man who performed miracles, died on the cross and rose again from the dead so we can have victory over sin and Satan.

Dear Heavenly Father, thank you that your Word does not come back void. Thank you for your promise to save and defend our children.

– Loretta Oppenheim

Daily Bible Reading Plan: Numbers 12-14; Mark 5

FEBRUARY 27

Christ's First Coming

"And they shall call His name Immanuel, which being interpreted is, God with us." Matthew 1:23b (KJV)

"And thou Bethlehem, in the land of Judah, art not least among the princes of Judah: for out of thee shall come a Governor, that shall rule my people Israel." Matthew 2:6 (KJV)

Many years before Christ came into the world as a baby, God had promised through the prophets that He would send a Messiah—a Savior—for the people, because they needed a way to get right with God. He told them that He would be born in Bethlehem, which was — at that time—a small town about six miles from Jerusalem.

There must have been many who knew what the Scriptures said, and some were actually waiting for Christ to come. But for the most part they were not concerned about it, as we see in the case of the priests and scribes that Herod spoke to. Even though they were told about a King being born in Bethlehem, the Scriptures do not tell us that any were concerned or excited about it. The Bible doesn't tell us that any of them were interested in making a short trip to find out if this was the One that their forefathers had been waiting for over the years. It did not seem to cause any excitement in the community at all.

However, it was different with the people who asked Herod where Messiah was to be born. These men had come many miles from the East in a caravan to worship Christ.

We can understand unbelief—as we see many in our day that are not concerned about the second coming of Christ, even though they have heard that He is coming again.

Lord, we pray that we will all take Your coming back seriously and be ready to meet You.

– Bill Jackson

Daily Bible Reading Plan: Numbers 15-16; Mark 6

FEBRUARY 28

Every Promise

"The Lord is faithful to all His promises and loving toward all He has made." Psalm 145:13B (NIV)

We need to be spending time in God's Word every day, claiming all these promises. It's a gold mine, and they are there for us to claim! Sometimes we tend to get discouraged and, for some reason, we choose to stay there. But if we get into the Word, it becomes hard to stay discouraged!

I remember there was a time when I was so hurt and discouraged that I found it next to impossible to read and pray, until I realized that I was just hurting myself more, and not having peace and forgiveness in my heart. I was letting the enemy win! So, I didn't stay in that rut. I climbed out, with the Lord's help, of course.

Sometimes when we pray, we wonder, "Does He even hear me?" or "Why doesn't He answer my prayers?" That's when we need to find the promises in the Word that pertain to what we are going through and make them ours. Keep praying and keep trusting!

As we get into the Word, it makes us better equipped to do His will, and better able to stand against what the enemy might throw at us. It helps us to be better able to help our children and to help others. Sometimes what we go through can be a real help to others. Usually, we think we're the only ones going through this hard time, but that is truly not so.

I would encourage you to read through the Bible in a year. As you read, at times the words just pop out to you, and it seems just what you need at that time. When these words and promises jump out at you, write them down, believe them and use them in your everyday walk. My main point is to *read* God's Word . . . so you can claim the promises! It's God's love letter to you!

– Pat Hall

Daily Bible Reading Plan: Numbers 17-19

FEBRUARY 29

God's Masterpiece – Orchids

"And why do you worry about clothes? See how the lilies of the field grow. They do not labor or spin. Yet I tell you that not even Solomon in all his splendor was dressed like one of these." Matthew 6:28-29

There are about 23,000 varieties of orchids. God must have been smiling while He designed these flowers. Some look like butterflies and others like braying donkeys with big ears. The flying duck orchid entices an insect to land on its scented head and then flips the visitor onto its back so that it picks up the pollen before moving on. The Lilliputian orchid is smaller than a pin, while a Cattleya species grows in huge clumps high up in the trees of Venezuela.

Some orchids look like a bushy-bearded hillbilly, and caterpillars like to crawl through the beard to pick up pollen for the next flower. Hummingbirds pollinate a little orange gnome looking character with a big hat. They find the nectar in the flower's mouth. An ugly black orchid that looks and smells like a female wasp is pollinated by a male wasp.

Madagascar has a white orchid that holds its nectar at the end of a foot-long spur. Scientists looked for years to find out what bird or insect could pollinate such a flower. They finally saw a huge moth with a foot-long proboscis that could unroll to drink the nectar.

The Peruvian bucket orchid doesn't look pretty, but it has an ingenious design. The insect lands on the scented, waxy lip; it then slips off into a bowl of liquid. Unable to fly out, it swims down to a little trap door and, as it wiggles through, it picks up a bead of pollen for the next flower. Isn't God amazing?

Dearest Lord, what a wonder You are! Thank You for displaying Your handiwork all around us so that we can better see who You are. Open our eyes so that we can better see You.

– Sue Carlisle

Daily Bible Reading Plan: Numbers 20-22

MARCH 1

Memories of Mom

"Her children arise up, and call her blessed; her husband also, and he praiseth her." Proverbs 31:28 (KJV)

My memories of my mother are good ones that I will treasure forever! I remember how us kids were the apple of her eye. Everything she did revolved around her family.

She always looked forward to Christmas and other holidays when the kids and grandkids would come home. She'd orchestrate huge meals, and nobody ever went hungry at her place! She'd cry for happiness when we came, and she'd cry again out of loneliness when we left (she'd start missing us a day before we were ready to leave!).

When Mom came to Jesus, it was also the start of a spiritual journey for each of us in the family. She passed her life teaching and being an example of faith to all of us kids. She loved the Lord so much and she never turned back from following Him.

Mom was real hard of hearing and, when it was time for devotions, she'd take her hearing aids out and tune out everything. She would read her Bible in peace while the whole house listened to her reading. I sure miss hearing that!

God really blessed Mom in her faithfulness to Him. She was a beautiful godly lady who drew respect from everyone who knew her. I know this sounds like a eulogy, but these are my memories of a lady that truly knew what it meant to live a life for Jesus. We sure miss you, Mom!

Dear Lord, thank You for my mother! In Jesus' name, Amen.

– Milly Jackson

Daily Bible Reading Plan: Numbers 23-25; Mark 7

MARCH 2

Let Go and Let God

"Therefore, as God's chosen people, holy and dearly loved, clothe yourselves with compassion, kindness, humility, gentleness, and patience. Bear with each other and forgive one another if any of you has a grievance against someone. Forgive as the Lord forgave you." Colossians 3:12-14 (NIV)

The bell had just rung at the elementary school. Recess was over, and it was time to go in. As I was one of the supervisors on duty, I assisted and followed the students going in, chattering playfully, and continuing to visit with their little friends. Except for two little girls.

I noticed there was an issue, so I went over and knelt down to speak with them to find out the problem. They both eagerly spoke at the same time almost in tears, as one was not wanting to be a friend anymore.

After a very brief intervention on my part, as we didn't have much time, I watched as both girls walked away hand in hand—no more tears, just in total friendship again, giggling happily as they rushed to their classroom.

Not only did this quick change of heart surprise me, but I realized that we as adults can learn a lot from children. Wouldn't it be nice if we could forgive as easily, and continue to love one another as God's Word has commanded?

I have learned that forgiving is a gift to myself and allows peace of mind. It is so much easier to let go and let God.

Father in heaven, help me to forgive others as You have forgiven me.

– Hazel Patenaude

Daily Bible Reading Plan: Numbers 26-28; Mark 8

MARCH 3

Expiry Date

"It is appointed unto men once to die, but after this the judgement."
Hebrews 9:27 (KJV)

I'm saying "good-bye" to a gospel musician friend of mine today. We'll be singing a few songs at his wake, and then the funeral is tomorrow. I'm really going to miss the guy! I'll remember him as one who lived his life victoriously.

Attending a funeral brings to mind our own mortality—something that most of us try to avoid thinking about until the harsh reality of it slaps us in the face. Like the milk carton in your fridge, you and I have an "expiry date." The biggest difference is that we usually don't know when that date is. All we can be sure of is what God's Word tells us in the above scripture. In other words, in this limited earthly timeframe, we are accountable for how we live our lives.

It kind of puts life in perspective when we look at things that way. Unlike your milk carton with an expiry date, we might not know when our time is done here, but we need to make sure that we are ready to meet God after that. Psalm 90:12 says, "Teach us to number our days, that we may gain a heart of wisdom." (NKJV) Settling things with God is something we need to look after in our time here on earth, not just "hope for the best" after our life here is over. God is so good!

– Kene Jackson

Daily Bible Reading Plan: Numbers 29-31; Mark 9

MARCH 4

Celebrating Christmas

"Today in the town of David a Savior has been born to you; he is the Messiah, the Lord." Luke 2:11 (NIV)

Sending us to Sunday school that first year prompted my mom to celebrate Christmas—something I didn't remember doing before. As she decorated the small tree, I asked her who God is. Her reply was simple, and something I have never forgotten. "God is someone who will never let you down. He will always be there for you."

She had been raised in the Catholic faith and sent to residential school. For her to know that and trust God was truly a gift for me and my siblings. It reminds me of Jesus' promise to never leave or forsake us (Deuteronomy 31:8).

I remember hearing the account of the angel appearing to the shepherds. The Bible says the glory of the Lord shone around them and they were terrified. The angel told them the good news about Jesus being born in the city of David, how they would find him in a manger. Then heavenly hosts appeared and praised God, giving Him glory, and saying peace on earth for men.

The Christmas songs described a beautiful scene and powerful words about Jesus being born. The star over Bethlehem, leading the three wise men to Him—all these vivid descriptions thrilled my young heart! The fact that our Lord and Savior was born in a stable gave me a humble heart and love toward Him. I really believe it also laid the foundation of how I would always want to celebrate Christmas, remembering it as the recognition of Jesus's birth. I love to sing the Christmas hymns.

Dear Heavenly Father, thank You for your gift of life through Your Son Jesus.

– Loretta Oppenheim

Daily Bible Reading Plan: Numbers 32-34

MARCH 5

No Harm Will Overtake You

"Because you have made the LORD, who is my refuge, even the Most High, your dwelling, there shall be no evil befall you, neither shall any plague come near your tent." Psalm 91:9-10 (MEV)

Because of my early life experiences, I carried fear into my adult life. As a young Christian, I did not realize that the enemy would use these fears against me. Often when alone, I would hear someone walking in the other room and, at night, I would see ugly faces in the windows. However, it was the evil presence I could feel around me that scared me the most.

A young summer missionary was living in our home at the time and noticed that I was struggling. He asked me if he could share my problem with the pastor and ask his advice. I said, "Sure." A few nights later the pastor and my sister and her husband came over to pray with me. God delivered me from the influence of the enemy that night.

The pastor encouraged me to fast, pray and commit scripture to memory. I chose Psalm 91. I was intrigued by the first verse: "I live within the shadow of the Almighty." God was standing over me, and I stood safe in His presence. Every verse in this psalm made me feel more secure in God's care.

However, verses 9 and 10 held a special promise for me after I learned that "The devil prowls around like a roaring lion looking for someone to devour" (1 Peter 5:8, NIV). This experience taught me that I need to know God's Word and become familiar with His promises to be ready for my fight with "unseen forces in the heavenly realms" (Ephesians 6:12).

Dear God, help me to remember that You are always with me and I do not have to face the enemy alone. Help me to remember that our enemy is an ever-present threat who comes to "steal and kill and destroy" (John 10:10).

– Theresa Bose

Daily Bible Reading Plan: Numbers 35-36; Mark 10

MARCH 6

Fear Not

"Fear not, for I am with you." Isaiah 41:10a (NKJV)

The phrase "Fear not" appears in the Bible many times, more than any other phrase.

It is strange that God has to remind us constantly not to be afraid. The Almighty God of the Universe loves us, and yet we are constantly afraid of a thousand things that might or might not happen. We need constant assurance that God loves us and is watching over us.

When my children were small, I would often hold them on my lap and read the Bible to them. We lived on a farm in Oklahoma and there were thunderstorms and tornadoes. One stormy night I was reading the Bible to my children and read, "Behold, I stand at the door and knock..." At that very moment there was a blinding flash of lightning and thunder shook the whole house.

My four-year-old son said, "Mom, I think Jesus is knocking on our door and you'd better let Him come in because He sounds mad!"

There is a lot to fear in the world—fires and floods, earthquakes, crime, tornadoes and hurricanes, disease and car accidents. The world can be a dangerous place. Every time we walk out the door, we risk not returning. We have plenty of reasons to be fearful, and one reason not to be fearful. God.

God holds us in the hollow of His hand. He loves us. He doesn't want us to be fearful or worried. He wants us to rest in Him, trust Him, and enjoy life. "The Lord is with me, I will not be afraid" Psalm 118:6a (NIV). "The very hairs of your head are all numbered. Fear ye not therefore" (Luke 12:7a, KJV). "Do not let your hearts be troubled and do not be afraid" John 14:27b (NIV).

God, forgive me when I worry about small things. Forgive me for not trusting You to take care of me.

– Crying Wind

Daily Bible Reading Plan: Deuteronomy 1-3

MARCH 7

Look at Who I Am

"For since the creation of the world God's invisible qualities—his eternal power and divine nature—have been clearly seen, being understood from what has been made." Romans 1:20a. (NIV)

Do you ever regret the choices you've made? Do you wonder if God exists and, if so, why you are in such a mess? Has a self-proclaimed Christian ever wounded you or led you astray?

My faith turned to rubble in 1990. I sifted through broken dreams and shattered trust, trying to find a solid foothold, but I kept slipping on fear, anger, confusion and shame. I lay on the floor crying out to God. I felt like I had a spiritual flu; I felt too heartsick to get up and function.

I had always tried to perform well and be a good Christian—only to discover how miserably I had been deceived and how terribly I had failed God and my family. Then, God gave me a different focus. I heard His gentle voice say, "Look at who I am."

I remembered Romans 1:20 and wanted to see Christ's nature and character. I began with the spectacular northern lights. The bush around me felt like a comforting blanket. I watched the beaver, birds, squirrels, and the occasional bear. I baked cookies and thought of all the foods, herbs and spices God gave us to enjoy.

He is artistic, generous, imaginative, and has a funny sense of humor. He created laughter and romance. If you are ever discouraged, look around and realize that He did not have to give us any of what you see. Even if you are in an unpleasant place, look at yourself with your beating heart and know that He has an amazing plan for you.

Lord, help each of us to look at who You are through what You have made. You are greater than any failure or any wound.

– Sue Carlisle

Daily Bible Reading Plan: Deuteronomy 4-6; Mark 11

MARCH 8

Seeing Myself

"You are the one who put me together inside my mother's womb, and I praise you because of the wonderful way you created me. Everything you do is marvelous! Of this, I have no doubt." Psalm 139:13-14 (CEV)

As a child I had difficulty in seeing value in my life. I looked at other people and compared myself to them. When I didn't think I measured up (which usually happened), I would look down on myself, thinking I was less than them.

That whole thought pattern followed me into my adult years. It took a long time before I realized that I was a real somebody to God!

Coming to that place brought a whole lot of changes in the way I looked at myself. I no longer saw myself as a "nothing." I felt valuable, like I had something to offer. I wasn't ashamed of who I was or wasn't. Knowing Jesus made all the difference in the world!

As I look back at the way I used to look at myself, I find it so different from my self-evaluation of today. I try to look at myself and see the person God made me to be, rather than the comparisons that I once used to base my self-worth on.

I thank the Lord for the transformation He brought into my life.

Dear God, thank You for how You've helped me see myself as worthwhile and valuable! Help me to never forget that! Amen.

– Milly Jackson

Daily Bible Reading Plan: Deuteronomy 7-9

MARCH 9

God Knows Best

"Then the Lord opened Balaam's eyes, and he saw the angel of the LORD standing in the road with his sword drawn. So he bowed low and fell facedown." Numbers 22:31 (NIV)

This story of Balaam, the donkey, and the angel (Numbers 22) reminds me that God knows best and prevents many things from happening that we do not know about. On a cold morning, my family and I were preparing to leave our Saskatchewan home for Manitoba. My van started, but there was no heat, so we ended up staying home.

Soon I started having chest pains. I called my daughter into the room. She started crying and called the ambulance right away. I was having a hard time breathing. I saw a very bright cloud coming towards me. I told my daughter, "I want to see Dad!" (my late husband).

Well, the next thing I knew I was revived. My daughter told me that my skin had turned grey and cold. I was released from the hospital a few hours later. A few days later I got into my van and cried out to God, "Father, this is your vehicle. I can't afford to pay any more big bills." It seemed like God was telling me, "Turn off the fan completely, then turn the key and start it." I started to pray, and then started it. I waited a few more minutes and then turned on the heat, and the fan started! I started crying and praising God and ran into the house. I told my daughter, "He did it again!"

"Mom, what is happening?" she asked. I told her, "God fixed my van. It's working!" She, too, was happy. If we would have gone to Manitoba that day, I probably would not be here today. Where we were to go, there were no hospitals or doctors close by. Sometimes God prevents us from dangers, whereas we do not understand why things occur the way they do.

– Liz Genaille

Daily Bible Reading Plan: Deuteronomy 10-12; Mark 12

MARCH 10

How Do You Take Your Coffee?

"There are different kinds of gifts, but the same Spirit distributes them. There are different kinds of service, but the same Lord. There are different kinds of working, but in all of them and in everyone it is the same God at work." 1 Corinthians 12:4-6 (NIV)

I was thinking about the different ways we do things. For us coffee drinkers, we seem to have a wide variance in the way we like our coffee. The coffee chain I gravitate to has four sizes of coffee: S, M, L and XL . . . three kinds of coffee to choose from: regular, dark roast and decaf . . . then they have sugar, cream, or sweetener options.

If you do the math, it comes out to 96 ways to build your own version, and that's not counting the double-double, triple-triple, and quad-quad variations! Yup, we all do things a little different, but the common denominator is that we're all coffee drinkers.

In the realm of the "Christ-Follower" community, we find huge differences in the group demographics. First Corinthians chapter 12 brings out the scope of the variances in nationality and social status . . . "Jews or Gentiles, slave or free—and we were all given the one Spirit to drink. Even so the body is not made up of one part but of many." (12:13b-14, NIV)

We are from such a mosaic of backgrounds, cultures, languages, and ethnicities. Our worship styles are all over the map and we embrace a range of doctrinal shades. We serve God in hundreds of ministry methodologies, but at the center of it all is our Crucified, Risen, and Reigning Savior, Jesus. We worship and obey Him as our Creator and Lord!

Next time you're in a coffee shop, eavesdrop and listen to all the ways people order their coffee. Springboard off that to consider the demographics, diversities, and differences among those with the highest privilege on earth, members of the gospel community . . . God's family!

– Kene Jackson

Daily Bible Reading Plan: Deuteronomy 13-15

MARCH 11

Strengthen That Which Remains

"Be watchful, and strengthen the things which remain, that are ready to die: for I have not found thy works perfect before God." Revelation 3:2 (KJV)

In Revelation 3, Jesus gave the church in Sardis a warning to repent and turn back to God. It sounds as if most of the believers in the church had become spiritually weak. But there is hope! . . . although death is mentioned, the possibility for renewal remains.

Some people have a life motto. My own motto is the title of this devotional. In our little village, language is what kept our people intact. That was a big part of our cultural identity, and the Oji-Cree dialect is what I speak. Many of our people were forbidden to speak our language in residential schools. I personally experienced this and could have lost my language, as many have. I was led to believe that there is something wrong with my language and, sadly, it impacted my life.

What kept reminding me of my language, though, was my father's teaching when he would sit me down at our kitchen table. He had me memorize the syllabic chart from his hymn book. I thank God for how He has helped me restore that part of my identity—today I speak and write my language. It's a blessing to worship God using the Cree hymn book. I encourage others to use our language any way we can, as it's quickly becoming lost, especially among our youth.

We all have beliefs and values that have defined us—especially how we walk with God. Are there other losses that we need to speak about? Perhaps godly lifestyles the church no longer practices? The Scripture states, "Be watchful and strengthen that which remains."

Let's take time to reflect and pray for what grieves us. Do our actions meet the requirements of our God? Let's go back to what we heard and believed at first and hold to it firmly. "Repent and turn to me," says the Lord.

– Liz Beardy

Daily Bible Reading Plan: Deuteronomy 16-18; Mark 13

MARCH 12

Lord, Use Me for Your Glory

"Who have been chosen according to the foreknowledge of God the Father, through the sanctifying work of the Spirit, to be obedient to Jesus Christ and sprinkled with his blood." 1 Peter 1:2 (NIV)

When the Lord first called me to His work, I was so excited and ready to go about sharing the Good News of Jesus Christ. But then things happened to destroy all that. I felt shame. There were people relying on me, but I had come up way short of everyone's expectations—most of all Jesus, who gave up all things for me.

I felt like an outcast. I sought to restore my relationships, but I remained hurt and angered because I was convinced that people did not understand what I was going through. I met with a Christian friend, thinking that he will be on my side and see things my way. After we talked quite a while, he said three words that angered me. Those words were, "You are selfish." But it was godly advice. My friend was telling me that I was serving myself and was sitting on the throne that was meant for Jesus.

All these devastating things that happened to me brought me into a closer relationship to Jesus. I had been placing "I" at the front, and not putting all things in His hands. First Peter 5:6-7 says "Humble yourself, therefore under God's mighty hand, that he may lift you up in due time. Cast all your anxieties on Him because he cares for you."

I prayed to God, saying I was sorry for serving myself, pleasing myself, and not placing God before me. Not many years after, the Lord opened a door of ministry for me once more. Praise God, I am still remembered by Him and have been restored for His glory!

– Ken Mitsuing

Daily Bible Reading Plan: Deuteronomy 19-21

MARCH 13

Never Hopeless

"The faithful love of the LORD never ends! His mercies never cease. Great is His faithfulness; His mercies begin afresh each morning. I say to myself, 'The Lord is my inheritance; therefore, I will hope in Him!'" Lamentations 3:22-23 (NLT)

The Bible is not clear as to the author of the book of Lamentations but, regardless of who wrote it, it appears to be someone who was in deep distress, particularly over the fact that Jerusalem was being destroyed by the Babylonians.

Imagine having your country and people in ruin! It is a terrible loss and the person who wrote this book shares what is going on.

The author was in deep distress, but was never hopeless. The author penned the words so beautifully, "The faithful love of the LORD never ends! His mercies never cease. Great is His faithfulness, His mercies begin afresh each morning."

That doesn't sound like someone in terrible ruin. Even though the author was in the midst of ruin, they put their faith and hope in the Lord. This encourages my heart to know that when discouraging times come (and they do), there is always hope!

It is hope that is certain and never wavers. God is in control of hard and discouraging times, and I know that I, too, can trust Him for the time and for the outcome.

– Myrna Kopf

Daily Bible Reading Plan: Deuteronomy 22-24

MARCH 14

Gospel Freedom—"Cast it off"

"And Jesus stood still, and commanded him to be called. And they call the blind man, saying unto him, Be of good comfort, rise; he calleth thee. And he, casting away his garment, rose, and came to Jesus." Mark 10:49-50 (KJV)

Life is unfair and hard at times. Unforeseen events, pain and tragedy seem to confront us. Events can prevent us from continual spiritual growth and happiness in our Christian life. Blind Bartimaeus begged daily in order to survive. During this time in history, such disabilities were often considered a death sentence. As a result, Bartimaeus was likely hopeless and broken.

We can all relate to spiritual captivity and bondage. Years pass by, and the wilderness season of spiritual drought drags on. The tendrils of doubt and discouragement take root deep in our hearts like Bartimaeus. However, with Jesus, what is impossible for man is not impossible for God! Hope rose in Bartimaeus's heart when he heard that Jesus was near. He began to cry out to Him for mercy, despite people telling him to be quiet.

Jesus stopped and called for Bartimaeus. Notice the Lord's compassion for this poor lost soul. Surely this was the best news that Bartimaeus had ever heard! Then, *casting away his garment, he rose and came to Jesus*, who healed him.

This is an incredible encouragement for us. No matter what mountain confronts you or bondage that besets you, cry out to Jesus! He will deliver you from the grip of the enemy. You may feel that you are all alone but, if you are a child of God, the Holy Spirit dwells in you. Jesus will never leave you nor forsake you. Arise like Bartimaeus. Cast away the lies, the discouragement, the shame, the anger and come to Jesus!

What has kept you defeated and discouraged? Jesus wants you to come to Him today and He can deliver you.

– Steven Keesic

Daily Bible Reading Plan: Deuteronomy 25-27; Mark 14

MARCH 15

Drops From Above

"If then you were raised with Christ, seek those things which are above..." Colossians 3:1 (NKJV)

The old trapper I was visiting mentioned "drops from a plane." I began to ask some questions of this man who had spent many years on a trapline north of Ft. Chipewyan, Alb.

He explained that it was difficult to take enough supplies to last for the duration of the winter and spring trapping seasons, so supplies were ordered whenever they ran low. Communication to the store was by two-way radio. People at the store would wrap up the order—things like flour, sugar, tea and lard. Then a plane would fly to the designated area and begin to drop the items. This worked well, as there were no nearby airstrips for landing and take-off.

Though this trapper had been familiar with this procedure for years, he remained fascinated with the accuracy of the drops. He said, "We never lost anything. As the plane circled, the carefully wrapped items would bounce near us until the drops were completed. They were right on!"

I had heard of similar things being done in other parts of the world. I felt there was a comparison here to something in the spiritual realm. Answers from God to us in "gift packages" should include the leading of His Spirit, more sound knowledge of His Word, and a genuine concern for others that moves us to pray for others and speak to them.

One more thing the trapper told me was, "When we came home from the trapline we went to pay for our drops from the plane." As believers, we know that we need not pay for our "drops from above"—they are gifts.

James 1:17 says, "Every good and every perfect gift is from above, and comes down from the Father of lights, with whom there is no variation or shadow of turning." (NKJV)

– Bill Jackson

Daily Bible Reading Plan: Deuteronomy 28-29

MARCH 16

Fried Bread

"The student is not above the teacher, but everyone who is fully trained will be like their teacher." Luke 6:40 (NIV)

Everyone always says, "My mom's fry bread is the best." I think back to when I would say the same thing. I can remember when I asked my mom to teach me how to make fry bread. She told my wife and me to grab a bowl, and she told us the ingredients: flour, water, oil, salt, baking powder . . . and two handfuls of love!

She told us to mix them together and try not to knead it too much. We would eventually fry it in oil that was in a frying pan, and it became a golden-brown masterpiece! She was a very good teacher.

The above Scripture reminds us of our need to be a student and to be taught. We are always students when it comes to the Holy Spirit, who is constantly teaching us to be fully mature. We can't be above the One who teaches us because the Teacher has been a teacher for a long, long time.

We may think that we know a lot, but do we really know a lot? When I first became a student of the Bible, it would come easy—but there is so much to learn about being a student for life.

The Holy Spirit was given to us so we can learn to be a believer, to learn to follow Him, and live a life that God wants us to live.

Living a godly life will teach you to be a good student, and one day you will be a teacher to another person, like my mother who taught me to make fry bread.

– Kirby James

Daily Bible Reading Plan: Deuteronomy 30-31; Mark 15

MARCH 17

Once Not a People

"But you are a chosen people, a royal priesthood, a holy nation, God's special possession, that you may declare the praises of him who called you out of darkness into his wonderful light. Once you were not a people, but now you are the people of God; once you had not received mercy, but now you have received mercy." 1 Peter 2:9-10 (NIV)

I grew up near Williams Lake, B.C., on a small reserve called Sugar Cane. I have many sweet memories of playing in the beautiful surroundings of my childhood home. When I started attending the Day School on the reserve, everything changed. The teacher was very cruel and racist. After completing grade six, I went off to residential school until I completed high school.

After these experiences, I had very low self-esteem and a deep confusion about authority figures. I started using alcohol and became dependent on it to boost my confidence and ability to interact with people. However, my sister gave her life to God and I noticed a change in her. She encouraged me to come to church with her. A missionary shared the gospel, and I put my trust in the Lord. In a study one night I heard, "You are a chosen people, a royal priesthood, a holy nation, God's special possession."

Those words did not fit my image of myself. I cried because I felt unimportant. God's Word was telling me something different. I was interested in learning more. Since then, I have learned how God sees me and about His love for me. John 3:16, 1 Corinthians 13 and Psalm 139 are only a few passages that tell us of God's love, His goodness, and His generosity.

Father God, I ask You to help me treasure the truths that Your word speaks, and to learn to apply these truths to my life.

– Theresa Bose

Daily Bible Reading Plan: Deuteronomy 32–34

MARCH 18

God Is Our Provider

"Jesus replied, 'They do not need to go away. You give them something to eat.' 'We have here only five loaves of bread and two fish,' they answered. 'Bring them to me,' he said." Matthew 14:16-18a (NIV)

We used to have Sunday school in our home back when we lived in Cormorant, MB. We had people from all ages attend. This one day, there were families from our community, and a lot of out-of-town families, too.

We used to feed the people who would come from out of town, but this day everyone decided to stay. We knew how much food we had, and it certainly wasn't enough food for everyone. My husband, Bert, and I talked it over and decided that he and I would not eat.

So, we prayed over the food that day. Everyone ate, and to our surprise there was some left over so Bert and I could eat after all. Wow!

It reminded me of the loaves and fish story in Matthew 14, where the disciples said, "We only have five loves and two fish," and Jesus replied, "Bring them to me." Do you know what happened? All the people had enough food that day, and there were even leftovers. There were over 5000 people to feed!

I believe that when we prayed over the food that day, God multiplied the food so everyone could eat. Praise Jesus!

Thank you, Lord, for hearing our prayers. You multiplied the food that day, and everyone including us had a meal! Increase my faith, Lord, to believe daily that You are Provider and will provide for my every need.

– Liz Genaille

Daily Bible Reading Plan: Joshua 1-3; Mark 16

MARCH 19

Power in Reserve

"I can do all things through Christ who strengthens me." Philippians 4:13 (NKJV)

I like my truck—it's a blue 2007 4x4 Chevrolet Avalanche. There's a bit of rust, a few years and a few miles on it, but it runs good and gets me around. When I'm cruising at normal speed on a flat highway, the 5.3-liter motor runs easily on four cylinders (using less gas). That's great as long as I'm not hauling a heavy load, trying to climb a steep hill, pulling a big old flat-deck trailer, trying to pass a semi-trailer—or all of the above (at the same time!).

At times like that, four cylinders just aren't enough. *I need more power!* It's then that all eight pistons cut in and you hear the mufflers ramp up to a "Harley-level" roar! My right foot sinks perilously close to the floorboard as it spurs my old Chevy into the next dimension (or at least past the semi)!

The verse above talks about those times when you need added strength to face bigger obstacles, harder situations, and more intense opposition than what your normal day brings. When your bank account is $6 overdrawn with no cheque on the radar . . . when "till death do us part" just walked out the door with a suitcase . . . when your doctor is making a living as the constant bearer of bad news . . . and when there's no sign that things will change anytime soon, you need strength to draw on that you just don't have in yourself.

When the road gets rough, I need my truck to go from four to eight cylinders and deliver that extra power I need *right now*. When my spiritual journey involves more mud, gravel and hills than level pavement, I need that added strength I'm promised in Philippians 4:13.

If the battlefield you're facing right now requires more spiritual stamina than usual, just know that it's there for you! As a Christ follower, you're promised and assured of His power *in all situations*.

– Kene Jackson

Daily Bible Reading Plan: Joshua 4-7

MARCH 20

Still a Chance

"Then he said, 'Jesus, remember me when you come into your kingdom.' Jesus answered him, 'Truly I tell you, today you will be with me in paradise.' " Luke 23:42-43 (NIV)

I remember visiting a home where the husband was dying from cancer. I asked if it was okay for me to go and see him in his room. The wife agreed. I entered the room, and you could tell that he did not have many days left. I asked him if he knew Jesus Christ, and he said he did not know.

I told him who Jesus is, and that He is preparing a place for us. I asked him if he would ask Jesus for forgiveness of his sins, and he agreed by nodding yes. I told him that he will be with Jesus in paradise for eternity, and he nodded yes. The next day he passed away.

When I think of this man, I think of the thief on the cross in Luke 23. One criminal defended Jesus and asked Him to remember him when He comes into the kingdom. The man in my story had not been a believer, but he became open to knowing Jesus. Like the thief on the cross he, too, had an opportunity to be with Jesus in paradise.

If you know someone who is close to death, they still have an opportunity to express their faith and not be led into the lake of fire. We all have a chance to "make it right" before we pass away, and it may take a believer in Jesus to make it happen. Don't let your loved one miss that opportunity. Tell them about Jesus and what to expect when they have no more breath. If you love them very much, take the risk. If they chose not to ask Jesus for forgiveness of their sin, at least you have made the effort.

– Kirby James

Daily Bible Reading Plan: Joshua 8-10

MARCH 21

Faith

"Now faith is the substance of things hoped for, the evidence of things not seen." Hebrews 11:1 (NKJV)

Scripture teaches us that no man has ever seen God. The only person to ever come close to seeing God that I read about in the Bible is Moses. And he only saw the back of God, not His face. God told Moses specifically how to approach Him. God said, "Stand in the cleft of the rock" and "you will see my back, but my face must not be seen" (Exodus 33:17-23). God told Moses in that encounter that no one had ever seen Him and lived. Why? Because that is the holiness of God. Incredible and powerful!

We can live our Christian lives three ways: by faith, sight, or good works. Here are reasons why I choose faith:

(1) We are instructed by the Word of God to walk by faith and not by sight (2 Corinthians 5:7). I am glad my Christian walk is by faith in God and not in people or things of this world. Guaranteed, people will disappoint you. But if your faith journey is in God, you will never be disappointed.

(2) What about good works? Well, doing good works is biblical, but even that can bring disappointment, frustration, and emptiness. The Christian life is all about balance. Absolutely, do good works, but don't make it the basis of your Christian walk. We do good works in ministry related to world disasters, overseas and local outreach to the poor in spirit. But remember, you and I must still rely on our faith in the Son of God. Hebrews 11:6 says, "Without faith it is impossible to please God."

Hebrews 11 is often called the "Hall of Faith." I encourage you to take the time to read it and be encouraged to see how the family of faith walked their journey here on earth and accomplished great things for the kingdom of God.

– Marshall Murdock

Daily Bible Reading Plan: Joshua 11-13

MARCH 22

Just Say No

"Let your yea be yea; and your nay, nay." James 5:12b (KJV)

It's hard for me to say "No." When I say "No" I feel guilty. I feel like I have to make excuses and explain why I can't do something, and I need to apologize.

When the minister of our church said he wanted to paint his house and needed volunteers to help him, I volunteered to help. I had expected about a dozen church members to show up, but I was the only one. His house was a small two-bedroom house. We started painting, and then he received a call and said he had to leave. I ended up painting the entire house alone—it took a week.

I spent 10 days taking care of the neighbor's cat while she visited friends in Utah. She said the cat was litter box trained. It wasn't. The cat was nervous, meowed constantly for its owner, and rarely used the litter box. When the neighbor returned, I didn't tell her about her cat, but the next time she asked me to take care of her cat I told her I was expecting company. I lied. I know I shouldn't have. I couldn't bring myself to be honest with her, and I couldn't just say "No." She never spoke to me again.

The list is endless. I have allowed people to take advantage of me for years, partly because I felt it was my Christian duty to help other people, and partly because I didn't have the courage to say "No" to anyone who asked for my help.

I don't regret the things I've done wrong as much as I regret the things I did right for the wrong reasons. It took me years to learn that sometimes it is alright to say "No."

Lord, give me the courage to say "No" when it is the right answer.

– Crying Wind

Daily Bible Reading Plan: Joshua 14-15; Luke 1

MARCH 23

Keep Generating

"Finally, my brethren, be strong in the Lord, and in the power of his might." Ephesians 6:10 (KJV)

A while back I was driving along during the evening. My headlights started dimming down, and the truck started to hesitate. We were still quite a way from home. The lights kept dimming down, and the truck would slow down. Every now and then we had to stop, and it seemed like the battery was draining.

Finally, we got home, and I realized what had happened. The day before I was working on the truck alternator, changing the brushes. So, I checked it and, sure enough, I realized that I had left the nail in the alternator that was holding up the brushes . . . so the brushes weren't seated. Because of that, the circuit was not complete, and we had an "unplugged" alternator.

I pulled out the nail, the brushes fell into place, and made the connection complete. It now worked fine and was now generating electrical power. Before, we were just running on battery power.

We must "keep generating"! It's a reminder to be plugged in, make contact, and keep generating. Isaiah in the Old Testament says that God helps tired people to be strong. He gives power to those without it. Even young men get tired and need to rest. Even young boys stumble and fall. But those who trust in the Lord will become strong again. They will be like eagles that grow new feathers. They will run and not get weak. They will walk and not get tired.

If you want light in your house night or day, the light must be plugged in. It must be plugged into the power source. The electrical plug is only a link to the power source, but a very important link.

For us to be in the place of light and power . . . we must be plugged into Jesus. Isaiah 2:5b says: "Let us walk in the light of the Lord." (KJV)

– Terry Hall

Daily Bible Reading Plan: Joshua 16-18; Luke 2

MARCH 24

Many Ways to Steal

"People do not despise a thief if he steals to satisfy himself when he is starving. Yet when he is found, he must restore sevenfold." Proverbs 6:30-31a (NKJV)

A supermarket manager rigs his scales to make customers' purchases appear to weigh more in order to overcharge them. God calls this "an abomination." Some otherwise honest folks boast about cheating on their taxes by inflating their tax deductions: "Hey, we're only working-class bums. Billionaires pay no taxes, so I hear."

But what does Scripture say about paying taxes? When the temple tax collectors come to Jesus, He honors their request and directs the apostle Peter to go to the sea, cast in a hook, and take the first fish. Inside its mouth will be a coin with which Peter is to pay the taxes for them both (Matthew 17:27).

Max, a little boy whose grandma has little money, gives him and his brother 10 pennies whenever they visit. The first 10 pennies go to older brother, Sam. Then Grandma counts what is meant to be 10 for Max. But Max notices there are nine pennies and a dime. "Grandma, you gave me too much," he says. "Thank you, son!" she says, and corrects the overpayment. On their way to the store, Sam grumbles, "You should have kept that dime!" Max shrugs, "Grandma might have needed it more." Which boy is more likely to grow up to be an honest person?

Margo wants money to see a movie. She steals the cash from her mother's purse. Is it okay to steal from your parents? What does the fifth Commandment say? Stealing also includes: kidnapping, taking an innocent person's life, gossip (which is stealing another's reputation), taking any property belonging to another, cheating a worker of his/her wages. How many more ways can you think of?

Father God, strengthen us to follow Your Word in times of our temptation. In Jesus' name, Amen.

– Kiki BelMonte-Schaller

Daily Bible Reading Plan: Joshua 19-21

MARCH 25

In the Blink of an Eye

"Be ye also ready: for in such an hour as ye think not the Son of Man cometh." Matthew 24:44 (KJV)

Back a while ago, we were having a conversation with one of our young grandsons about Jesus Christ coming back for us. He was sitting in a big chair, looking up into the sky for a while, when all of a sudden he said, "Jesus is coming, Jesus is coming!"

We said, "Where?" He pointed out the window and, at that moment, a big jet was flying over. As it passed by, he said, "Jesus left us behind."

After it had passed and disappeared, we said, "Jesus is not coming by plane, train, or car. But he will come in the blink of an eye. So, he blinked and said, "Boy, He is taking a long time."

He had thought that Jesus was coming that day, and he wanted to be ready. Later, we noticed that he was actually watching by the window with his coat on, waiting for the return of his Lord and Savior.

We told him again, "When Jesus comes, just blink and you will be in Heaven that fast." So, he blinked again, then said, "But I'm not in heaven."

We do not know the time or day when He will return. But we can be vigilant and wait on the Lord's return. We can have faith like my little grandson, watching, expecting and knowing that He is coming.

Lord, we do not know the time or day when You will return. We don't want to be caught unaware and unprepared. Help us to remain vigilant and wait on Your return.

– Liz Genaille

Daily Bible Reading Plan: Joshua 22-24; Luke 3

MARCH 26

Doors

"Trust in the LORD with all your heart, and do not lean on your own understanding. In all your ways acknowledge him, and he will make straight your paths." Proverbs 3:5-6 (ESV)

I took the time the other day to count the doors at our place. It took about 30 seconds to figure out that there's 12 of them. Kind of a mundane exercise, but it got me thinking about "closed and open doors" and how God uses both kinds in our lives.

The "open doors" are the opportunity ones. They can be captivating, motivating and exciting or, on the flip side, intimidating, overwhelming, and downright scary! You see, open doors usually mean "change." Change is a great concept, but most of us are wired to resist it.

The "closed doors" are more of an enigma. Sometimes it's an issue where we've had a real brilliant, "Einstein-ish," "Mensa-grade," "Humdinger" of an idea, only to find that nobody else shares our enthusiasm . . . that finances aren't there, and logistical realties (or common sense) present us with a closed door.

It's not an exact science, and it takes a lot of prayer to differentiate between "normal" obstacles and doors that are truly closed, but as we follow God's way and get to know the principles and absolutes of the Scriptures, it gets easier to make those distinctions.

As we seek guidance in our lives from God's Spirit, we learn that two of His navigational tools are open and closed doors.

– Kene Jackson

Daily Bible Reading Plan: Judges 1-3; Luke 4

MARCH 27

Why Should I Be Afraid?

"And the very hairs on your head are all numbered. So don't be afraid; you are more valuable to God than a whole flock of sparrows." Luke 12:7 (NLT)

As a child and teenager, I used to think that God was distant—that He created this world and left. My mom started going to a church in our community, and it was quite obvious that there was a change in her life. She shared with us that she had become a Christian.

I didn't understand what that meant, but I did see the change in her life. She wanted to know more about God, and a friend told her about a Christian Native school not far from where we lived. It was called Key-Way-Tin Bible Institute, near Lac La Biche, Alb.

Next thing, my mom and siblings were on their way, moving to live at Key-Way-Tin. However, I went to live with my uncle in the city because I didn't want to be at a Christian place. But things didn't work out with my schooling in the city, so I moved back with my mom to take classes in Lac La Biche, which meant living at Key-Way-Tin.

As I lived with Mom and my siblings, she would share some of the Bible truths that she was learning. There was no doubt that she was thoroughly enjoying studying God's Word. She shared with us the gospel and different stories from His Word. One Bible passage that stood out to me was in Luke 12:7, stating that the very hairs on my head are numbered! Wow! That really intrigued me. I thought God was distant, but Him knowing even the number of hairs on my head made me realize that He is not distant at all.

Not only is God personal . . . He is relational. He is a loving God who knows me so personally, more than I will ever understand, and values me so much! Why should I be afraid?

– Myrna Kopf

Daily Bible Reading Plan: Judges 4-6

MARCH 28

Grandma Without Fear

"So do not fear, for I am with you; do not be dismayed, for I am your God. I will strengthen you and help you; I will uphold you with my righteous right hand." Isaiah 41:10 (NIV)

I remember years ago when we were coming up the fishing trail, bringing our well-caught deserved river salmon home. I was with my grandmother, and there were two other children who were ages seven and nine. I was nine years of age.

For some reason our dogs did not go with us that night. That night we met a bear on the trail! It put so much fear in us that we almost tore my grandmother's clothes off of her clinging to her!

Grandmother was calm as a cucumber and spoke words in our language. The bear left us alone and left the area. I am not sure what she said, but that bear listened. (Interestingly, I found out later that we are from the Bear clan!) Whatever the reason the bear left us alone, I know that my grandmother was my hero at that moment.

The Scripture above tells us that we should not fear, for God will always be there for you. You should not have to worry about anything because He's got you. It was like my grandmother. She was there when we needed protection from fear. She just spoke and the bear left.

I truly, truly believe that is all the Lord has to do—to speak, and the fear will leave us. He has us with His righteous right hand. Think about it—one hand, not two! So, when it comes to struggle with fear, remember that He is always going to be there for us.

It was during that time when my grandmother was starting her path as a believer, and I am certain she placed her faith in the Lord.

– Kirby James

Daily Bible Reading Plan: Judges 7-8; Luke 5

MARCH 29

Feisty

"Look at the birds of the air; they do not sow or reap or store away in barns, and yet your heavenly Father feeds them. Are you not much more valuable than they?" Matthew 6:26 (NIV)

Who of you by worrying can add a single hour to his life? Luke 12:25 (NIV)

I often remember Feisty, a little squirrel with a notch missing on his ear, who visited our yard in northern Alberta. Our cabin was located along a migration path and, in spite of the frigid temperatures, many birds wintered there. Hundreds of pine grosbeaks, evening grosbeaks, redpolls, gray jays, and chickadees visited our yard daily.

Feisty took ownership of the feeders that we filled from a 50-pound bag of sunflower seeds stored near the patio. His greatest challengers were the blue jays. Feisty raced from one feeder to the other, chasing away the jays. His eyes sparkled with the challenge; his little tail waved as a banner of his success. Then he scurried back to fill his cheeks with seeds and ran to deposit them in his private store—our bag of sunflower seeds. Over and over he rushed back to the feeders, chasing the jays and filling his storehouse.

I don't know if he realized that, as he chased one group of jays far out into the yard, another group swooped in to eat at the feeders. Then, as soon as Feisty ran for his stash, the chased group came back to eat. We laughed at him, but it made me wonder if my flurry of activity amuses my heavenly Father.

Dear Father, thank You for sharing Your wisdom with us through the antics of a small squirrel. Help us to listen to Your voice as You direct our days so that we will not get sidetracked with our own ambitions and plans that end up in futility. Help us to lean not on our own understanding, but to rely on You in all that we do.

– Sue Carlisle

Daily Bible Reading Plan: Judges 9-10

MARCH 30

Casting It All

"Casting all your care upon Him; for He careth for you." 1 Peter 5:7 (KJV)

I always liked this verse, but I never really understood it until I watched some fishermen casting their nets into the water. The men waited patiently for the right waves to come rolling in, then they would take their circular nets that had weights around the edge and, with all their strength, they would cast their nets out into the water.

The word "cast" had a new meaning. They threw their nets into the waves, and they cast them away as far as they could. They let go of their nets. When the nets sank, there would be fish caught in the nets and the fishermen would haul them back and remove the fish. The men did this over and over. They were strong men, but it must have been exhausting to cast the nets out and then haul them back when they were full of fish. Many of the disciples were fishermen—tough, muscular, strong men who worked hard pulling in nets full of fish and casting the nets out again over and over.

They didn't toss the nets, or let the nets float away, or let the nets sink to the bottom. They used all their strength to throw the nets as far as they could, to cast them away.

I wanted to cast all my cares on God. I wanted to use all my strength to throw them as far away from me as I could—casting them away forever, never to think about them or worry about them or grieve over them again.

The Bible says, "casting *all* your care." It doesn't say some of your care, or part of your care—it says *all* your care . . . care about your family, health, finances, job, marriage, children, problems . . . *all* your care.

I will cast all my cares on God. I will let go and I will not remember.

– Crying Wind

Daily Bible Reading Plan: Judges 11-12; Luke 6

MARCH 31

Resurrection Sunday

"Jesus said to her, 'I am the resurrection and the life. The one who believes in me will live, even though they die.'" John 11:25 (NIV)

A couple years back, about a week before Easter, a fellow musician shared with me this viewpoint on Easter Sunday. I'd like to pass it on to you. Read on . . . he said, "I don't call it *Easter Sunday* anymore. I call it *Resurrection Sunday*. Why? Because every time I say that I'm telling whoever's listening that Jesus is Risen—that He's Alive!"

Just by naming the day in that manner, he was testifying to everyone in his world that he believed in a Savior who was alive. After mulling that over for a while, I decided to start calling it that, too!

I was reading some from J. F. McArthur's writings and came across a really good resurrection quote: "If He never rose, He wouldn't be alive. If He wasn't alive, He couldn't give us life. But He did arise, and He said in John 11:25, 'I am the resurrection and the life; whoever believes in Me even though he dies, shall live again.' So eternal life is dependent upon the resurrection."

He's not "just" risen. Look at what Ephesians 1:20-22 (NIV) says: "He raised Christ from the dead and seated him at his right hand in the heavenly realms, far above all rule and authority, power and dominion, and every name that is invoked, not only in the present age but also in the one to come. And God placed all things under his feet . . . "

No, He's more than just risen. The Word says, "... far above all rule and authority, power and dominion . . . " He's absolute deity! Not just risen! He's Lord of All! On Resurrection Sunday, that's the One we honor; that's who we're focused on!

— Kene Jackson

Daily Bible Reading Plan: Judges 13-15

APRIL 1

Never Alone

"Fear not, for I am with you; be not dismayed, for I am your God. I will strengthen you, yes, I will help you, I will uphold you with My righteous right hand." Isaiah 41:10 (NKJV)

Nothing in this world can give us the confidence and security that we need. Only God the Father can. Only God can do this, as He is the one who can give us His presence for eternity, wherever we go and whatever we do.

Therefore, I will not fear whatever comes. I will keep my eyes on Him. I know He will lead me in the very best way possible.

After my husband died, I wondered, "How am I ever going to survive without him? Am I ever going to be able to go out on ministry again, alone?"

I was scared to go alone, as the memories and thoughts of singing together and traveling to places together flooded my mind. "I'll have to drive alone by myself," I thought.

Then God's Word came to me from Isaiah 41, a reminder that I do not have to be afraid, and that God will strengthen me.

Praise God for His Word and His precious promises. I can have confidence in my God in everything I can do for Him. I don't have to hide away in my closet and grieve. Yes, I have my grieving and my time of crying, missing my beloved husband, but I also have my joy in the Lord.

Father, the joy of the Lord is my strength, for in my weakness I am made strong in You. You have been my Shepherd, led me beside still waters and never left me alone. Thank You for comforting in my grief. And thank You for encouraging me to not stop sharing your love with others.

– Liz Genaille

Daily Bible Reading Plan: Judges 16-18; Luke 7

APRIL 2

Using Our Gifts

"Each of you should use whatever gift you have received to serve others, as faithful stewards of God's grace in its various forms."
1 Peter 4:10 (NIV)

The early believers were learning how to uplift and encourage each other through the use of their individual gifts. Peter was writing to them to instruct them further in this area.

This reminds me of a little girl who always wanted to help. Anything she could do for somebody, she would do it. Whether it was helping her mom with the housework, or looking after her brothers and sisters, she was always there. She didn't know at the time that her Bible called this the gift of helps.

As she grew up, she found that she still liked to help people and, as she began to seek out her spiritual gifting, it turned out to be the gift of helps. She became a singer, and did a lot of counseling, as the doors opened for those opportunities.

That little girl was me! I never realized that I had something to offer God. I was really shy and had a very difficult time to interact with people, much less counsel them!

As I grew in the Lord, He transformed my thinking and my outlook on life. It was then that I was able to start using my spiritual gifting to help and encourage other people. What a joy!

Dear God, You have given every one of us different gifts to serve you with. Thank You for the gifts You've given me. Help me to use them to honor You! In Jesus' name, Amen.

– Milly Jackson

Daily Bible Reading Plan: Judges 19-21

APRIL 3

Gifts from Above

"Every good and perfect gift is from above, coming down from the Father of the heavenly lights, who does not change like shifting shadows." James 1:17 (NIV)

Often when we experience big tests, trusting God is not our first reaction. Then God speaks to our spirit and directs us to His Word.

When more cancer was found in my system and I needed a second surgery, I was angry. Angry with the surgeon for not getting all the cancer the first time, angry that I was going back into surgery in two days and, yes, I think I was angry with God for my circumstance.

I left to visit my brother who lived about three hours away. On the way, "Every good and perfect gift comes down from the Father of lights, who does not change like shifting shadows" popped into my mind. I did not know the reference, so I Googled it and found it in James. I was amazed that God spoke so clearly to me. He reminded me of where my experiences were coming from and that they were good. That scripture brought peace to my heart.

God taught me many lessons in that season of my life. I gave up my job and lost my regular income, and my body was changed forever. In retrospect, I realized that these "things" had taken my focus away from God. I had given a lot of my time to perfecting my job, and I often wasted my earnings on frivolous, prideful buying.

In the early months of my illness, I was afraid and unsure of the future, so I immersed myself in God's Word. I spent many hours in prayer. I learned about His "rest" (trusting that He has me and is in total control of my circumstances).

Father God, thank You for getting me back on track with You and teaching me that I can trust You in every circumstance.

– Theresa Bose

Daily Bible Reading Plan: Ruth

APRIL 4

Pride and its Consequences

"Pride goes before destruction, and a haughty spirit before a fall."
Proverbs 16:18 (NKJV)

It's late afternoon. Jack, a bright all-around student, dribbles his basketball on his family's driveway. He stops, aims at the net above the garage door, and shoots. A three pointer! There is no one to celebrate with him, so Jack whoops and dances around. A car pulls up. His friend, Dan, starts toward Jack.

"Whatzup?" Jack asks in familiar slang as he continues to dribble the ball. "The debate team is meeting in a half hour. Can you come? We found out that Sohi College dropped out and we'll be debating that tough Citywide College team on Friday. We need to get together. One of the subjects is climate change. There's lots of research we need to do.

Jack sinks another three-pointer. "Wow! You see that? It's my third money ball today. For sure, I can go pro some day!" "Yeah, if you grow another six inches," Dan chides. "Now, what about debate practice? You coming? We need you, man. I told the team I'd pick you up and bring you."

"I don't need to practice," Jack replies. "I can out-debate anybody, any place, any time. I'll be there Friday for sure, okay? Have I ever let my team down?" "But what about that climate change topic? It can go a dozen ways, so let's get going on the research. You're our top debater, Jack. We really need you, man!" Dan pleads.

Friday arrives. The rival teams are seated on stage. The moderator introduces them. The debate is on. But because Jack's pride in believing himself unbeatable and too smart to need study and practice, he seems unfocused and cannot refute his rivals. His team loses.

"Humble yourselves under the mighty hand of God, that He may exalt you in due time" 1 Peter 5:6 (NKJV).

Father God, grant me humility in my thoughts, words and actions, that I may be pleasing in Your sight. In Jesus' Name. Amen.

– Kiki BelMonte-Schaller

Daily Bible Reading Plan: 1 Samuel 1-3; Luke 8

APRIL 5

Prayers Not Answered

"But whoever lives by the truth comes into the light, so that it may be seen plainly that what they have done has been done in the sight of God." John 3:21 (NIV)

A woman had prayed and prayed for her children to turn from their ways of addiction. She even asked the church for prayer that God would help her children stop and turn from their ways.

It was for about seven years that she continued to pray, and it seemed nothing was happening. She slowly stopped coming to the church. We think she has given up on God because her prayers were not being answered.

Let me share some Scripture that might help us understand this story. John 3:19-21 in another translation says, "They are judged by this fact: The light has come into the world. But they did not want light. They wanted darkness because they were doing evil things. Everyone who does evil hates the light. They will not come to the light, because the light will show all the bad things they have done. But anyone who follows the true way comes to the light. Then the light will show that whatever they have done was done through God." (ERV)

God does hear and answer prayer. He wants to and is willing to work with this woman's children. But everyone has a free will provided by God. In her case, it seems that her children are not ready to give up the darkness they are living in and choose to stay in that lifestyle.

Everyone who loves evil hates the light, and that is the truth. The ones who are true believers love the light. This woman's children need to see the light of Jesus and turn from their darkness. Sad to say, many can't see beyond the darkness they are living in.

Let's keep praying. God waits for people who are living in darkness to come to Him.

– Kirby James

Daily Bible Reading Plan: 1 Samuel 4-7

APRIL 6

Faithful Servants

"Therefore go and make disciples of all nations, baptizing them in the name of the Father and of the Son and of the Holy Spirit." Matthew 28:19 (NIV)

I will never forget my mom putting us five kids to bed early on a Saturday night because we were going to go to Sunday school the next day. My six-year-old thoughts were, "What!? Why? It was our day off from school."

A faithful man named Mr. Staley from the Oakridge Baptist Church in Vancouver had been visiting mom, explaining the Christian faith to her. He was obeying Jesus's words from Matthew 28:19. I'm reasonably sure he came at least three times to talk to her about sending us to Sunday school. As I reflect on these times, I can't help but think there must have been a lot of people praying for her to say yes. As it was, she only sent my older sister and I because the others were too young.

I expect it took some extra encouraging, since mom was a survivor of residential school—something she never talked about to any of us. It has made me believe that mom had a faith of her own, in spite of what she may have experienced or witnessed in residential school. She was a peaceful person, gentle, caring.

Nevertheless, Sunday school was where I first learned about God and Jesus. Sunday school was a safe place, bright, full of love and learning, and exciting stories. We memorized verses, earned Bibles, and went to Bible camp. I really looked forward to going every week. A family came to pick us up every Sunday until we were old enough to take the bus. I am forever thankful for these faithful followers reaching out to our family.

Dear Heavenly Father, thank You for Your servants who brought us to Sunday school where we learned the Good News about Jesus and came to believe.

– Loretta Oppenheim

Daily Bible Reading Plan: 1 Samuel 8-10

APRIL 7

Is Any Sick Among You?

"Is any sick among you? Let him call for the elders of the church; and let them pray over him, anointing him with oil in the name of the Lord: And the prayer of faith shall save the sick, and the Lord shall raise him up; and if he has committed sins, they shall be forgiven him."
James 5:14-15 (KJV)

I was about 12 when I got stricken with a very bad skin disease. I missed a few of months of school and was eventually bedridden as the disease progressed. In my little village in northern Ontario, medical facilities were scarce. My mother was my main caregiver. Some kind neighbors would bring remedies, but they did not help.

One day my mother came home from church and told my father that she had invited elders from the church to come and pray for me. That evening they arrived with their guitars and Bibles. They sang songs and read Scripture. They asked if I could be seated on the sofa, and they gathered around me. The pastor anointed me with oil, and they prayed as they laid hands on me.

I found myself weeping as a sweet presence came over me. I got up from the sofa and was instantly healed by the power of God! I was sent out to a nursing station, examined, and they could not find anything wrong. The disease never came back.

I met the Lord Jesus as my Healer that night when those men of God honored God's Word . . . to pray for the sick and they shall be healed.

Sadly, many churches don't follow the Scripture. Many have created their man-made rituals or religious practices to deal with the sick. I share my testimony of healing to encourage believers to honor God's Word, such as stated in James 5:14. God honors our faith in Jesus.

– Liz Beardy

Daily Bible Reading Plan: 1 Samuel 11-12; Luke 9

APRIL 8

Maskepetoon—Peacemaker

"Peace I leave with you; my peace I give you. I do not give to you as the world gives. Do not let your hearts be troubled and do not be afraid." John 14:27 (NIV)

I've been intrigued by the story of a Rocky Mountain Cree of the mid-1800's, a chief named Maskepetoon. Told by many, it has become a mix of myth, legend, and truth. However, all sources mark the man with the common denominator that follows the common thread of "Peacemaker."

Maskepetoon, a renowned warrior who came to faith in Jesus, found out that personal peace could only come when it was partnered with forgiveness. His only son had been murdered by a companion. Maskepetoon, faced with the choice of killing or forgiving him, offered his forgiveness to the man.

His own dad had been killed by a fighter from another tribe. Years later, Maskepetoon met this warrior and extended his forgiveness to him, inviting him into his lodge and presenting him with a garment.

But peace isn't desired by all. Peace doesn't come easily, and peace doesn't come cheap. Maskepetoon paid the ultimate price when he later entered an enemy camp unarmed to negotiate a peace treaty. He was killed by a fighter from there.

It seems rather ironic that his pursuit of peace would cost him his life. In Maskepetoon's eyes, the reward was worth the risk—the payoff was worth the price. Maskepetoon and his peacemaking endeavors were rejected by those around him but, if you had asked him, it was worth contending for!

– Kene Jackson

Daily Bible Reading Plan: 1 Samuel 13-14

APRIL 9

God is True to His Word

"Because of the LORD's great love we are not consumed, for his compassions never fail. They are new every morning; great is your faithfulness." Lamentations 3:22-23 (NIV)

Isaiah 55:8, 9 has stuck out to me throughout the years. It really helps me put in perspective how great and wonderful and all-knowing God is. "For my thoughts are not your thoughts, neither are your ways my ways," declares the Lord. "As the heavens are higher than the earth, so are my ways higher than your ways and my thoughts than your thoughts." (NASB)

These verses have taught me not to question what happens, but to ask God to show me what He wants me to learn. The reason I chose the title is because when child killer Clifford Olsen let the world know he had found God through Jesus, our neighbor Monty was outraged and asked me how God could forgive Clifford and take him in? "What kind of God is that?" he demanded to know. My answer was, "One true to His Word. Wouldn't you want that?"

It was amazing that this same child killer had stayed in the home of my husband's supervisor who had two daughters around the age of Olsen's victims. The father was a believer and prayed every night that God would protect his girls, not even suspecting that the man he was showing God's love to was a murderer. There were times Olsen was left with the girls while their parents went to take care of something. He behaved as an ordinary man, playing with the girls, taking care of them. There was no reason for the father to suspect Clifford to be a danger to his daughters. God protected them through this time!

Heavenly Father, thank You that You are never changing, the same yesterday, today, and tomorrow. I can trust You every minute, every hour, every day.

– Loretta Oppenheim

Daily Bible Reading Plan: 1 Samuel 15-16; Luke 10

APRIL 10

Ungratefulness—A Hard Pill to Swallow

"Surely the righteous shall give thanks to Your name" Psalm 140:13a (NKJV)

There are few things more painful than doing someone a kindness and having them treat it with disdain. After working in secret for weeks, Margaret, a prize-winning bead crafter, has finally finished the intricately beaded vest for her daughter, Princess. She wraps it and places it beneath their Christmas tree.

When the big day arrives, Margaret can hardly wait to see Princess's eyes brighten when she sees the vest! But when her daughter unwraps the gift, she scowls and tosses it back into the box. She says, "Here, sell it at the next powwow! I'm not a bead wearing Rez girl! I deserve designer threads like the girls wear at school!" Margaret can barely hold back her tears.

In Exodus 14, God—through Moses—parts the Red Sea so that the Israelites can escape Pharoah's pursuing army bent on returning them to Egypt and slavery. Yet, once on dry ground, their constant grumbling against God and Moses rouses God's anger. He punishes them by extending their time in the wilderness.

Ten lepers see Jesus and cry out for Him to have mercy on them. Jesus tells them, "Go, show yourselves to the priests." They obey. Each realizes he is healed, but only one is so grateful that he returns, glorifies God, and falls on his knees before Jesus in thankfulness. "Were there not ten cleansed? Where are the nine?" Jesus asks the onlookers. "Were there not any found who returned to give glory to God except this foreigner?" Luke 17:14,17-18 (NKJV)

In giving thanks it shows that we remember God's goodness and the kindness of others. We must never forget to give thanks for what is done for us.

Thank You, Father God, for Your goodness toward us through Your precious Son, our Lord and Savior, Jesus Christ. Amen!

– Kiki BelMonte-Schaller

Daily Bible Reading Plan: 1 Samuel 17-18; Luke 11

APRIL 11

Compassion One For Another

"For God so loved the world, that He gave His only begotten Son that whosoever believeth in Him should not perish, but have everlasting life." John 3:16 (KJV)

A. God loves us. This is only one of the Scriptures that tells us that God loves us. Not just me. He loves all of us, the whole world. He loves not just the good people, but also the bad people. Drunks, alcoholics, drug addicts, murderers, thieves . . . all sinners are loved by God. God doesn't love the sin, but He loves the person He created.

Psalm 97:10 says, "Ye that love the LORD, hate evil: He preserveth the souls of His saints; He delivereth them out of the hand of the wicked." (KJV)

B. God looks after us. Remember that God created you and He loves you. He will not let anything happen to you that He does not will. If something bad happens in your life, don't try to wonder why. It may be God's way to use you later on in life to share with others who have or are going through the same or similar trials or tribulations.

C. God allows hard time to strengthen us. God always has a reason for allowing us to go through trials in our life—to strengthen us and to use our testimony of how we handled it with God's help. We are always to ask our Heavenly Father God for help to deal with our problems. We are to lay our burdens on Him to take care of. He wants to help us and take care of us if we call on Him. Just remember He is always there waiting on us to ask. He always wants to help take care if we ask.

Dear Heavenly Father God, may my request be of Your desire to receive what is needed, also to seek what You desire in my life as I walk with You and for You. Amen.

– Ed Bird

Daily Bible Reading Plan: 1 Samuel 19-21

APRIL 12

Be With Him

"And He goeth up into a mountain, and calleth unto him whom he would; and they came unto him. And He ordained twelve, that they should be with him." Mark 3:13, 14a (KJV)

Recently, a teenager had been attending our small church faithfully for two months, but he suddenly stopped. About a month later I saw him walking with a friend. I asked him why he stopped coming and he replied, "I have been very busy and don't have the time." His friend piped up, "He is always busy on Sundays."

My wife and I wondered what could keep a 13 year-old so busy that he did not have one hour? We marvel that, despite the age, the justification is often the same: "I don't have time for God." This is one of the devil's most effective tricks. Our enemy will attempt to do anything to keep us from spending time with Jesus. If a lamp is unplugged from the wall, the bulb loses the power to light up a dark room. Similarly, to live a victorious and overcoming life, we must continually spend time with Jesus by reading the Word of God and developing a prayer life.

Throughout the years I have noticed that peace and joy in Christ consistently reigns in my life as I faithfully spend time with Jesus. In Mark, we see that Jesus desired to be with his disciples and "that they should be with him." Friend, notice that before they were sent forth to preach, heal sickness, to cast out devils with great power and authority (vv. 14,15), they were to "be with Him."

Spending time daily with Jesus is the key to conquering every bondage, hindrance, sin, discouragement, and depression. Spending time with Jesus will transform our lifestyle, behaviors and attitudes. Transformation happens by simply "being with Him" each day.

Do you spend time with Jesus every day? Isn't it amazing that Jesus desires you to *be with Him*?

– Steven Keesic

Daily Bible Reading Plan: 1 Samuel 22-24

APRIL 13

Going Through It with Me

"Therefore, it was necessary for Him to be made in every respect like us, His brothers and sisters, so that He could be our merciful and faithful High Priest before God." Hebrews 2:17 (NLT)

The High Priest mentioned in this verse is Jesus! In Philippians 2:6-7 it says, "Though he was God, he did not think of equality with God as something to cling to. Instead, he gave up His divine privileges; he took the humble position of a slave and was born as a human being. When He appeared in human form . . ." (NLT)

God humbled Himself and became like one of us. He experienced pain, loneliness, and rejection from those who were close to Him. Because he deliberately experienced these painful emotions, He is able to understand what we go through and sympathize with us.

There is an old Native saying: "Take the time to walk a mile in his moccasins." Well, in this case, Jesus walked more than a mile for us. He walked and carried a cross on His wounded body to Calvary to die on that very cross.

But on the third day He rose from the dead! He is now, as the Bible says, our "merciful and faithful High Priest before God."

Not only does God understand me fully, but He is more than willing to help me when life gets hard—when I go through times of testing, He guides me through it. I am not alone—He goes through it with me as my merciful and faithful High Priest, a Priest above all priests.

– Myrna Kopf

Daily Bible Reading Plan: 1 Samuel 25-26; Luke 12

APRIL 14

An Undivided Heart

"I will give them an undivided heart and put a new spirit in them; I will remove from them their heart of stone and give them a heart of flesh. Then they will follow my decrees and be careful to keep my laws. They will be my people, and I will be their God." Ezekiel 11:19-20 (NIV)

It is easy to allow habits to creep in and take up residence in our lives just as the Israelites did in Ezekiel 11. We can allow the world around us to sell us their idols. Our focus becomes our jobs, our sports, our cars, or any other thing that starts to absorb our time and affections. Then God will intervene and allow circumstances in our lives to bring our hearts back to Him.

As a child, I dreamed of becoming a teacher. Life circumstances prevented me from realizing my dream. Still drawn to this environment, I volunteered in schools until I got my first job as a classroom assistant. Years later, when my children were grown and my husband agreed, I went back to school. After earning my degree, I was thrilled to have my first class. Having my dream job added a new dimension to my life. After 15 years, though, I started to feel exhausted all the time. Two years later I received a diagnosis of cancer. The initial shock, followed by a fear of death, caused me to seek God.

I spent many hours in study and prayer. I realized that my heart had become calloused. More of my time and attention was going to my teaching. Revelation 2:4b-5 (NIV) says, "You have forsaken the love you had at first. Consider how far you have fallen! Repent and do the things you did at first."

Father God, help me to keep my focus always on You. Thank you for blessing my life with Your goodness, Your healing, my family, my church family, and Your many answers to prayer.

– Theresa Bose

Daily Bible Reading Plan: 1 Samuel 27-29

APRIL 15

Realizing Potential

"Do not be conformed to this world, but be transformed by the renewal of your mind, that by testing you may discern what is the will of God, what is good and acceptable and perfect." Romans 12:2 (ESV)

It just sits there. There's an old 1964 Mercury "Shorty" school bus behind my dad's place that's been sitting there since 1976 when one of my brothers blew the motor on it. It's a sweet little three-window bus that I sometimes wonder what it would take to fix up, rebuild, restore, and customize . . . it would sure turn heads as it chugged down Main Street!

Problem is, it's just "potential." It's just a thought of "what could be." It may happen someday, or maybe it will just sit there and rust 'til it's deemed as scrap iron.

It kind of reminds me of us as people. God gave each of us a certain amount of potential—things that we are capable of, things that we could be, ways that God could use us, ways that we could maximize what we have going for us right now, ways to become what we are designed to be.

Problem is, it's just "potential" until we start to let God have his rebuilding, restoring, recreating hand in our lives. It's only then that we begin to see the new person that God can morph us into.

It's only then that our potential can translate to reality.

– Kene Jackson

Daily Bible Reading Plan: 1 Samuel 30-31; Luke 13

APRIL 16

He Knows Your Needs

"But seek first the kingdom of God and His righteousness, and all these things shall be added to you." Matthew 6:33 (NKJV)

When I attended Key-Way-Tin Bible Institute in the early 1990s, I began to learn what it means to trust in the Lord for everything. To get a diploma, three years were required. I did not know how I was going to pay for the three years. I was out of high school and didn't have a job.

I gave my life to Jesus on January 14, 1994, and the Bible school staff graciously worked it out so that I could start after the spring break. I just knew in my heart that God wanted me there to study His Word and learn to grow in Him. So, I didn't have much money to my name, but I had a rich Heavenly Father!

One time I badly needed new glasses, as mine were slowly falling apart. I was thinking that I would have to put duct tape on them, as I was desperate and can't see anything without my glasses. It didn't reach that point, though. In church one Sunday I came across this Bible passage (printed above). I *was* seeking God's kingdom, and verse 32 of the same chapter says, "Your heavenly Father already knows all your needs."

Yes, even if it's new glasses! After church one Sunday, I decided to take a nap. During the nap, I heard some footsteps by my door, but nobody knocked or said anything. On the floor underneath the door was an envelope that read "God Bless." I opened it up and there was 250 dollars cash! A gracious couple drove me to the city where I had an appointment with the optometrist. I picked out the frames that I liked. When I paid for it, the total cost was $249.99! Yes, I just had enough. God knew what I needed, and He sure provided!

– Myrna Kopf

Daily Bible Reading Plan: 2 Samuel 1-2; Luke 14

APRIL 17

Flight

"Trust in the LORD with all your heart and lean not on your own understanding. In all your ways acknowledge him and he will make your paths straight." Proverbs 3:5-6 (NIV)

Imagine we are living in the 1700s. We've carried water from the lake or creek, chopped wood for the fire, and started a stew for supper. (You men brought game home yesterday.) How difficult would it be for us to believe the tale of an odd-looking stranger who shows up with a wild story about a machine called a "747"—that we can walk into, with all of our luggage, find a seat with a window, and look down as it lifts us high into the thin air and carries us across the ocean?

This is the same air that we breathe. We can wave our hands through it. How can a plane lift thousands of tons into that flimsy air? We have all seen airplanes and many of us have traveled in them, but I still can't get over the wonder of it. My husband used to fly small planes, and he explained the aerodynamics of the wind over the wings. But, really, I don't think I could believe it could be done unless I saw it for myself.

Walking with God is a bit like this. We can't see Him—like we can't see the air—but we can see and feel the result of His presence. If we lean on Him—even when we don't understand everything—He will lift us up. He will comfort and guide us. He will give us wisdom on how to walk with Him through this life on earth. He accomplishes what is impossible for us.

Thank you, Lord, for the wonders You gave us on earth. Thank You for caring about each of us and having a design for our lives as awesome as flying through invisible air. Please open our eyes and hearts so that we can see and understand Your ways.

– Sue Carlisle

Daily Bible Reading Plan: 2 Samuel 3-5

APRIL 18

Clocks and Watches

"But they that wait upon the LORD shall renew their strength; they shall mount up with wings as eagles, they shall run, and not be weary; they shall walk and not faint." Isaiah 40:31 (NKJV)

I remember the first time I heard someone say, "I have a watch that does not have to be wound up every day; it runs by a battery." In those days our watches and clocks didn't have batteries to run them—they had a spring inside that was turned and turned until it was tight. Then the "time teller" was ready to go for another day.

I still have a clock that works with a spring. Personally, there is something I like about the ticking of a clock. The old clock can teach us something. If you do not wind it up each day, it will not tell the truth; it will not point the right direction, and it will lose time.

The believer in Christ should take time each day to worship the Lord in devotions, reading and prayer. If a believer does not take these times of worship, they will be like a spring clock that has not been wound. They will go slower and slower and soon will not be pointing in the right direction by his life.

It is very important that we spend time with the Lord each day. We need to be renewed in our spirits each day, as we see in the Scripture verse above, and in Psalm 39:4a: "Lord, make me to know my end, and what is the measure of my days." (NKJV)

Lord, help me to know that I need to spend time with You, so that I can be heading in the right direction.

– Bill Jackson

Daily Bible Reading Plan: 2 Samuel 6-8

APRIL 19

When Next Door Neighbor Knows Best

"Train up a child in the way he should go, and when he is old, he will not depart from it." Proverbs 22:6 (NKJV)

"Mama! Danny's throwing rocks at that cat again!" Maya calls out, then says to her brother, "How come you keep throwing rocks at him? He's not bothering anybody!" "Cause I hate cats! Next time, I'll get my BB gun and that'll take care of him!" says Danny. Mother answers from the doorway, "You shoot that cat and we'll be in big trouble with Tribal Police! Now go get washed up for dinner!"

The children scurry inside just as Miss Easter White, their next-door neighbor, comes over, leaning on her cane. "I want to talk to you for a minute, Thelma," she says. "Come in," she replies. "Have some dinner with us." "Not today, thank you. I heard what's happening between Danny and that cat. It's good you told him what might happen if he shoots it."

"Absolutely! I told him I can't have him getting us in trouble! His daddy should never have bought him that gun. Guns aren't toys and should never have been made as toys!" Miss Easter answers softly, "But I never heard you tell him such talk is wrong. I have two cats of my own. Bring Danny over. He'll see how they play with toys and can even open doors. Danny needs to see there's more to cats than walking across his yard."

"I'll ask him if he wants to go watch your kitties. No sense sending him over if he's only gonna cause you problems." Miss Easter smiles and replies, "When it's between right and wrong, you 'tell' children, not 'ask.' I'll look for him tomorrow—with ice cream for a treat!"

"A righteous man regards the life of his animal" Proverbs 12:10a (NKJV).

Our Father in heaven, grant that we, too, regard all that You have made as "very good."

– Kiki BelMonte-Schaller

Daily Bible Reading Plan: 2 Samuel 9-11; Luke 15

APRIL 20

Hiding God's Word

"Your word I have hidden my heart, that I might not sin against You." Psalm 119:11 (NKJV)

I remember memorizing Psalm 23 in Sunday school. That earned me my first Bible! I like that the teacher said memorizing Scripture is like hiding God's Word in our hearts. As I grew older, I realized what a treasure God's memorized Word is.

Keeping God's Word with us this way serves in several ways. It is a reminder to not sin against Him and to draw on His many promises. It also helps us to be encouraged in moments we may experience fear and doubt. We also memorized the 10 Commandments and the Lord's Prayer. I was 12 when I walked to the front to accept Jesus as my Lord and Savior.

I remember my sister getting up and walking to the front. I had heard the choice so many times—"Accept the Lord Jesus as your personal Lord and Savior and go to heaven or die without Him and go to the eternal lake of fire." (We weren't allowed to say "hell.") I decided to accept Jesus—being in eternal pain wasn't what I wanted. After hearing about Jesus' love for all of us, over and over again, it was a clear choice. The pastor's wife asked me if I was just copying my sister. I absolutely was not! The choice was all mine.

The 10 Commandments became more important, and had more meaning, as did the Lord's Prayer. Psalm 23 is good to gather strength from, and I always encourage others to read it when they are discouraged or have lost their way for a moment. Isaiah 55:8-9; Romans 8:38-39; 1 Corinthians 13; Jeremiah 29:11 . . . I have not fully memorized these, but often refer to them. This is one of my goals, to memorize more.

Dear Heavenly Father, thank You for Your precious Word. Help me to hide more of it in my heart.

– Loretta Oppenheim

Daily Bible Reading Plan: 2 Samuel 12-13; Luke 16

APRIL 21

Getting Past Anxiety and Worry

"Do not be anxious about anything, but in every situation, by prayer and petition, with thanksgiving, present your requests to God. And the peace of God, which transcends all understanding, will guard your hearts and your minds in Christ Jesus." Philippians 4:6-7 (NIV)

Growing up in my little community, I lived with a lot of anxiety. It seemed that I was worried about everything. I'd fret over things at school, things at home, and almost every aspect of life. One of the ways that I dealt with my anxiety was trying to control situations I faced. That approach didn't work very well, but that was the only way I knew of.

Even after I gave my heart to the Lord, it was still a difficult area. When I got married, the control issue was a problem. The fear and uncertainty of growing up in a home where alcohol was center stage really impacted my outlook on life.

As I grew in the Lord, I began to understand that I could leave everything in God's hands! I didn't have to worry about things or try to control my life situations.

First Peter 5:7 says, "Cast all your anxiety on Him because He cares for you." (NIV)

It's been a learning process, but it's so good to know that God cares about every detail of our lives!

Dear God, thank You that when I become anxious and worried about things in life, I can always come to You. You are faithful and just and You've shown me that I can leave my burdens and cares with You. Thank You that I don't have to carry them on my own! Amen.

– Milly Jackson

Daily Bible Reading Plan: 2 Samuel 14-15; Luke 17

APRIL 22

Praying in Jesus' Name

"You are from God, little children, and have overcome them; because greater is He who is in you than he who is in the world." 1 John 4:4 (NASB)

Years ago, back in northern Manitoba, we met a young teen girl who was desperately asking for help. There were three of us in the home at the time, and she had been lying down in one of the rooms when she asked for help.

So, I went in there, and prayed for her. As I knelt down beside the bed and began to pray, the other person in the home came in. The teen girl looked at him and said, "I will kill you!" She said this in a voice that didn't sound at all like her.

The young man ran out of that room so scared. As for myself, I was scared, too, feeling like the hair on the back of my head stood up. I felt such an evil presence there, but I just stayed on my knees and kept praying.

Maybe a half hour went by as I remained on my knees beside her, when all of a sudden, I felt a gust of wind fly by and out of that room. I felt the presence of the Holy Spirit of God, then peace and quietness.

The young girl said, "Help me get rid of my rock and roll cassette tapes." So, we went and threw them in the outhouse hole (we should have burnt them instead).

You see, as followers of Jesus, we have been given authority, by Him, in our battle with the enemy. When we pray in Jesus' name, we can have confidence that He is fighting our battles for us.

Father, thank You that You are King of Kings and Lord of Lords. Thank You that You are more powerful than any enemy we may fight. As we face difficult situations, help us to "Be Still" (Psalm 46) and pray in the name of Jesus.

– Liz Genaille

Daily Bible Reading Plan: 2 Samuel 16-18

APRIL 23

God at Work

"And we know that God causes all things to work together for good to those who love God, to those who are called according to His purpose." Romans 8:28 (NASB)

When you experience hard things in life, it is difficult to believe that God has anything to do with what is happening. Early in my Christian walk, my older brother died a violent death at the hands of another family member. This was the first death in my immediate family that I had experienced.

I went through many emotions during that time. It was a big test on my faith in God. I did not know where my brother was because I did not know for sure that he was born again. I was horrified and crushed at how his life ended. I felt helpless to be of any assistance to his family and my parents.

Because of my confusion, I looked for answers from several mature Christians. One pastor read Romans 8:28 to me. I was upset and asked him, "How can any good come from such a horrible incident?" He encouraged me to go home and meditate on that scripture. I read Romans 8. Many verses stood out to me, but I tried to apply verse 28 to my family situation. After a time, I still did not understand it, but decided to believe what it says.

It was then that God reminded me how He had kept my sister-in-law's faith strong throughout the weeks following her husband's death. She had even encouraged others around her in their faith. Then later, both my parents put their trust in the Lord. Since then, I have seen God's goodness in many situations.

Father God in heaven, please help me to remember, You work for the good of those who love You and have been called according to [Your] purpose.

– Theresa Bose

Daily Bible Reading Plan: 2 Samuel 19-20; Luke 18

APRIL 24

Be Ready

"You also must be ready, for the Son of Man is coming at an hour you do not expect." Luke 12:40 (ESV)

One of my most difficult things in life is "time." I think about when I would get to my doctor's appointment just one minute before my appointment. I was worried that if I was late, I would have to pay the $50 charge for being late.

I think about it when I am to meet a client for a meeting, and I just make it on time. I tend to forget that rush hour or lunch time rush could play a factor in my plans to get from point A to point B.

Some use the excuse of "Indian time." But if you really think about it, Indians were always on time when it came to gathering food, preparing for the seasons, and making sure that their communities had all their needs met. I am talking about back in the day.

What I am driving at is that we need to process our time to ensure that we are not late for something very important . . . and we won't have to regret the outcome. I am referring to our Lord's return. If we continue to just sit back and not do anything to get ready, we might miss the gates closing on us, and Jesus will say, "Do I know you?"

We need to be ready and to be on time when He comes. He will come unexpected and, if we are not ready for Him, we will be disappointed. We need to prepare ourselves for when He comes. We need to repent of our sins, accept Him as our Lord and Savior and follow Him all of the days of our lives. And when He comes, we will be ready and on time. It's like the Native people who gather all their provisions for the winter and prepare for any hardship it brings. We need to be ready for the second coming.

– Kirby James

Daily Bible Reading Plan: 2 Samuel 21-22

APRIL 25

This Side of Heaven

"We know that God causes all things to work together for good to those who love God, to those who are called according to his purpose." Romans 8:28 (NASB)

On this side of heaven, we may never understand how all things can work together for good for God's children. If we trust God, He will turn all these into opportunities for spiritual growth.

My daughter and I both had dreams of a very dark storm coming our way. I believe God was preparing me for what was coming. My husband had been sick for a few weeks and had lost 27 pounds. He was admitted to the hospital with pneumonia and COVID-19. Since there were restrictions, it meant that none of us could be with him.

Every day I phoned him to read the Bible and pray. I felt the dark cloud hovering over our home, and I couldn't eat. When I didn't have the appetite to eat, I would force myself. Without warning he was transferred to Saskatoon. None of us were allowed to go with him. He had to go alone in the ambulance. This would be the last time that I saw my loving husband, as a few days later he passed away.

Yes, I was shocked and devastated. I couldn't cry. I just felt numb. One moment I was happy he wasn't suffering anymore, the next moment I was angry at the medical people. All of a sudden, I felt God's peace like I never felt before. He was telling me, "I am here, and you will see him again soon."

I am thankful for my Heavenly Father and the Word of God. Yes, I have times when I cry and grieve, but I know that my husband would not want me to stay in my closet and waste away. He would say, "Liz, go out there and tell them about our Great Savior Jesus." I am blessed as I go out and minister for Jesus.

– Liz Genaille

Daily Bible Reading Plan: 2 Samuel 23-24; Luke 19

APRIL 26

Mountain Rock—God's Reminder

"I will set you up on a high rock where your enemies cannot reach you." Psalm 27:5

"When my heart is overwhelmed; lead me to the rock that is higher than I." Psalm 61:2b (NKJV)

Our village is surrounded by beautiful mountains. A huge rock on one mountain sits by itself on top—a reminder from God in different ways. For one, it weighs tons. No one carried it up there, and no one can take it down! God placed it there. Nothing is too hard for Him. It's a reminder that He is the Rock—the Rock of all Ages.

It's also a reminder that when you stand on that rock, you will see things in a new perspective. It's a reminder that you are standing on a solid foundation—Jesus Christ Himself being the chief cornerstone (Ephesians 2:19-22). The rock is also a reminder that God is Alpha and Omega—without beginning or end. For centuries people have been born and have died. Yet that rock still sits on top of that mountain. It's a reminder that God is the same yesterday, today and forever.

As the stars are God's handiwork, so is that rock. The Creator put it there so that I could tell you about it today. Only a few people know about it. I have touched it, stood upon it, and prayed. As I look down from that rock to our village, it speaks to me about the Kingdom of God. Again, it reminds me that God is all knowing, all powerful, and everywhere.

When you become a Christian, you won't live on a perpetual "high." The psalmist went down to the very depths, and so did the Apostle Paul. But in the midst of all circumstances, God's grace, peace and joy are there. The tears will still come, the pressures will be felt, and so will the temptations. But there is a new dimension—a new direction and a new power in your life to face your circumstances.

– Terry Hall

Daily Bible Reading Plan: 1 Kings 1-2

APRIL 27

Biblical Advice for Grief

"God blesses those that mourn, for they will be comforted."
Matthew 5:4 (NLT)

God knows you will experience grief in this life, but you're not meant to go through it alone. Relying on God and others can relieve your sorrow. Ecclesiastes 3:1a-4 says: "To everything there is a time . . . a time to weep . . . a time to mourn, . . ." (KJV) John 11:35 says, "Jesus wept." (KJV) Jesus felt deeply the pain of Lazarus' death.

I was raised in a culture where open grief was not normal. I recall standing by a family that had suffered a devastating loss to suicide. While viewing the casket, a little girl was weeping. A grandmother beside her was trying to comfort her by telling her not to cry. I can only imagine how the girl felt. From then on, she may have believed that it was not okay to cry.

I have heard many stories of grief and loss as a counselor. Most often I hear symptoms such as, "It's like something is stuck in my throat." True sorrowing is a normal stage of grief, which is a deep gut cry. To cry is very therapeutic and brings an emotional release from pain.

This taboo—"don't cry"—was broken in my village years ago when we tragically lost a young man. During the wake service, the church was packed. A respected elder of the church got up and stated that we had suffered a devastating loss, "But it's okay to cry." It was like a dam broke—everybody was crying, from youth to adults. As one of the crisis workers, we didn't know what to do. We tried to comfort everyone, then finally one of the workers said, "It's okay, let them grieve."

Today, I am very grateful for the freedom to grieve with others and to comfort those that mourn. But most importantly, Jesus Christ is the greatest Comforter—He modeled grief by weeping. He is also the Healer. Psalm 147:3: "He healeth the broken in heart, and bindeth up their wounds." (KJV)

– Liz Beardy

Daily Bible Reading Plan: 1 Kings 3-5; Luke 20

APRIL 28

Giving Over to God

"Don't lay a hand on the boy!" the angel said. "Do not hurt him in any way, for now I know that you truly fear God. You have not withheld from me even your son, your only son." Genesis 22:12 (NLT)

Not too many people like tests. The test that Abraham had received was a hard one—it was a testing of his faith. In Genesis 22:2, God tells Abraham to, "Take your son . . . Go and sacrifice him as a burnt offering on one of the mountains."

The next morning Abraham and his son head out. The fact that Abraham listened to God, and did what was required without complaint, challenges me. This was his only son who he deeply loved. Yet the story ends happily as God stops Abraham provides a ram as a substitute sacrifice. Now that was a test of faith in God!

There are times when I have had to give over to God what is precious in my life—to say, "God, this is not mine . . . this loved one does not belong to me but belongs to you. You can do whatever needs to be done."

A test for me was giving my family over to God. As a young adult, I would get very lonesome if I was away. Yet I wanted to be a missionary, and that would require being away from family, maybe a long distance.

When I read about Abraham, it comforted me and gave me hope. When I give my family and other cares into His capable hands, God will take care of it. I just need to have my hands open and say, "God, You know what is best. Do as You please in this situation."

Today I have been away from my family, living across Canada, and now in the States. Not once have I felt homesick. God truly has answered my prayer in giving my family over to Him. He has given grace that has been enough!

– Myrna Kopf

Daily Bible Reading Plan: 1 Kings 6-7

APRIL 29

East and West, North and South

"There is a way that seems right to a man, but its end is the way of death." Proverbs 14:12 (NKJV)

Do you know the four directions? Some people do; some people don't. I think those who don't know stand a chance of having difficulty getting to their destination, that is, if finding a place depended on knowing which way is which.

A man was going to a city 120 miles east and was told to go south until he reached the main highway, then turn left. Then he was told, "You can't miss it." He did reach the main highway but turned right instead of left. It wasn't until he reached another city 100 miles in the opposite direction that he realized that he was now at least 200 miles from where he wanted to go!

The Bible talks about a way that people follow, thinking that they are on the right road, but actually they are on the wrong road, away from God. Our verse for today, Proverbs 14:12, says, "There is a way that seems right to a man, but its end is the way of death."

It would be foolish of a person not to try to find out if he is going to heaven or not. After all, eternity is not like a few years in jail, or some kind of detention. A person who does not have the Savior in his life will be away from God forever and ever.

Make sure you have Jesus in your life. He is the One who said, "I am the way, the truth, and the life" (John 14:6, NKJV). Have you made sure of your eternal destination?

Lord, please show me Your Word. Help me listen to what it says so I will know where I am going. Save me, so I will not go in the wrong direction.

– Bill Jackson

Daily Bible Reading Plan: 1 Kings 8-9

APRIL 30

A New Creation

"Therefore, if anyone is in Christ, he is a new creation. The old has passed away; behold, the new has come!" 1 Corinthians 5:17 (ESV)

I was born as a Cree person, and I am very proud of who I am. I was raised by my mom and dad with values and virtues. There has been a lot of talk lately about "finding yourself" in order to be healed. I was never healed because of who I was, but by the saving grace of God the Creator, who through His Son Jesus Christ, saved me from eternal separation from God.

God gave me a new living hope and transformed me from within. I let go of the old nature, but I never lost my identity as a Native person when I came to Christ. In the Word of God, I am called a new creation. This verse does not say I am no longer a Cree person who gives up my language and culture, but God starts dealing with the sin in my life and begins the process of sanctification. This will never stop until the day the Lord returns, or I am called home to be with the Lord forever.

The above Scripture talks about God giving me a new life because I have put my faith in Jesus Christ as my Savior who died for me on the cross to pay my penalty of sin. Acts 4:12 says "Salvation is found in no one else, for there is no other name under heaven given to mankind by which we must be saved."

God changes my life internally and externally and sets me apart for His glory. When we become new creations, the Holy Spirit leads, guides and teaches us through the Word of God to live our lives holy unto the Lord and sets us apart for His glory to represent Him, and to honor Him with our lives.

– Ken Mitsuing

Daily Bible Reading Plan: 1 Kings 10-11; Luke 21

Our Contributing Writers

(in first name alphabetical order)

Abraham Jolly

Abe and his wife, Linda, live in Mistissini, Quebec, where he has served as the Director General of the Cree School Board. Abe is a member of the Mistissini Cree Nation. He has earned an honorary doctorate from Briercrest, loves to sing, and his music is appreciated by many.

Bill Jackson

Bill is from Whitefish Lake #128 First Nation, Alberta, where he lives with his wife, Shirley. Bill has served as a missionary, pastor, Bible teacher, radio & television speaker, and author. He is a founding member of Native Evangelical Fellowship of Canada (NEFC).

Crying Wind

Crying Wind is a longtime contributor to *Intertribal Life* newspaper, and has published several books, including bestsellers *Crying Wind* and *My Searching Heart*. She continues to engage readers with her simple honesty. April has been a widow for 25 years.

Ed Bird

Ed is a member of Ahtahkakoop Cree Band, Treaty 6 Territory, where he has Elder status. Before his struggles with health, he worked as a truck driver and retail meat cutter. Now he helps his sons with cutting up game.

Frank Ward

Frank and Lori Ward live in Lac La Biche, Alberta, where Frank pastors the nearby Kikino Bible Church. He loves teaching God's Word and outreach to the surrounding Métis community. Frank is from Loon River Cree First Nation, Alberta. The Wards have two teenage children.

Jennifer McEwen

Jennifer lives with Ken, her husband of 26 years, in the community of Xaxli'p, near Lillooet, British Columbia. She is from the St'at'imc Nation. For five years she has managed the St'at'imc Christian Homeschool, working to build Christian character in the lives of young people.

Hazel Patenaude
Hazel is Métis and resides in Buffalo Lake Métis Settlement, about two hours northeast of Edmonton, Alberta, and is employed in the community of Boyle.

Ken Mitsuing
Ken and his wife, Erna, belong to Makwa Sahgaiehcan Cree Nation (Loon Lake, Saskatchewan), where he has Elder status and works as Band Manager. Ken has been serving as a teaching elder in the local fellowship.

Kene Jackson
Kene is Plains Cree from Whitefish Lake #128 (Goodfish Lake). He serves as Executive Director of Native Evangelical Fellowship of Canada, with Freedom River Counselling Group, and travels extensively in music ministry with his wife, Milly.

Kiki BelMonte-Schaller
Kiki is a member of the Cherokee Confederacy Tribe. She contributes a column to *Intertribal Life* Newspaper, focusing on accomplished Indigenous/Native American women. She resides in South Florida with her husband, Jim.

Kirby James
Kirby is from the Shackan Band of Nlaka'pamux Nation in British Columbia. He is a former social worker, now serving as pastor of New Life Fellowship in Prince Albert, Saskatchewan. He and his wife, Bernadette, have a teenage son.

Laurie Wood Ducharme
Laurie is a member of St. Theresa Point Anishininew First Nation and lives in Winnipeg with her husband, George, and their son. She is Acting Chair of First Nations Community Church, sits on the Board of Inner-City Youth Alive, and is involved with Ashawaabic Ministries.

Liz Beardy
Elizabeth (Liz) is Oji-Cree from Bearskin Lake First Nation, northwestern Ontario. She was a social worker for 13 years before training to become a counselor in 2000. She resides in Sioux Lookout, Ontario, working in counseling/mental health ministry under a tribal council.

Liz Genaille
Liz is Cree, a member of Pimicikamak First Nation in Manitoba. She served in full-time ministry with her late husband, Bert, for many years in local church and music. Now based in Nipawin, Saskatchewan, Liz finds continued opportunities to share her faith through testimony and music.

Leana Patenaude
Leana is Métis and resides in Buffalo Lake Métis Settlement, about two hours northeast of Edmonton, Alberta. Leana is Hazel Patenaude's daughter, another writer in *Council Fire*, and works in administrative support.

Loretta Oppenheim
Loretta married into Coldwater Band (Interior Salish), Merritt, British Columbia. Her mom was from Chawathil Band (Stòlo Nation), and her dad was Cantonese, first generation born in Canada. Loretta works for an Indigenous child welfare agency as an administrative assistant.

Marshall Murdock
Marshall was raised on Fisher River Cree Nation (Treaty 5, Manitoba) and is semi-retired from work in corporate retail, banking, insurance, accounting, and administration. He has served on the Indian Life board and in local church leadership. He and his wife, Thelma, live in Winnipeg.

Milly Jackson
Milly and her husband, Kene, have their home in southern Alberta, but spend much time traveling in music evangelism ministry. She grew up in the Métis community of Cormorant, Manitoba, and through marriage is a member of Whitefish Band #128 (Alberta).

Myrna Kopf
Myrna is Cree from Buffalo Lake Métis Settlement, northern Alberta. She has taught at a Native Bible school, then served with a Christian publisher. Myrna is married to her husband, Joel, residing in Idaho where she works at a care center for elderly with alzheimer's and dementia.

Pat Hall

Pat and her husband, Terry, are from the Nuxalk Nation Band on British Columbia's west coast. After living in Vancouver, they moved back to Bella Coola in 2010. Serving as members of North American Indigenous Mission (NAIM), they are involved in church planting and radio outreach through NEFC.

Rose Buck

Rose Buck is a member of Opaskwayak Cree Nation (Treaty 5) near The Pas, Manitoba. She is a ministry worker with Native Fellowship of Canada (NEFC), assisting in a local fellowship along with NEFC publications work and conference planning.

Steven Keesic

Steven's past work includes practicing law and directing an addictions ministry center. Steve, who is from Lac Seul First Nation in northwestern Ontario, and his wife, Noemi, are currently pastoring in Lac Seul in association with Native Evangelical Fellowship of Canada.

Sue Carlisle

Sue is from the Ponca tribe of Nebraska but grew up on Wind River Reservation in Wyoming. She lives with her husband, Wes, in Thunder Bay, Ontario, and is a regular contributor to *Intertribal Life* newspaper. She serves with NorthWind Family Ministries Learning Centre.

Theresa (Terry) Bose

Terry and her husband, Bill, reside in west-central British Columbia. She is a member of Secwepemc First Nation, Williams Lake Indian Band, and has been employed as a schoolteacher since 2000.

Terry Hall

Terry and his wife, Pat, are members of Nuxalk Nation and reside in Bella Coola, British Columbia, serving in association with North American Indigenous Mission (NAIM). Terry has worked as an electrical engineer and has served in Native Evangelical Fellowship of Canada (NEFC) leadership.

In Appreciation

Indian Life Ministries wishes to thank the numerous ministries and individuals who made *Council Fire* possible. Whether through prayer, finances, contribution of content, or the offering of wisdom and experience, you know who you are and we appreciate you.

Thank you for reading *Council Fire, Volume 1*. We pray that it has encouraged you, and will continue to do so as you may choose to use it again next year. Or you may want to share it with a friend. Please write to us and let us know how the devotionals have helped and challenged you.

Did you know that Indian Life Ministries has many more great resources filled with encouraging stories and help? We also print a newspaper—*Intertribal Life*—filled with positive Indigenous news and gospel truth. You can have it delivered to your postal address.

Contact us:

Toll-free: 1-800-665-9275
Email: director@indianlife.org
Website: www.indianlife.org

In Canada:	In the United States:
Indian Life Ministries	Indian Life Ministries
PO Box 94	PO Box 32
Langdon, AB T0J 1X0	Pembina, ND 58271